The Double Helix-DNA

OUR DESTINY

Predestination

القدر

AHAMED KUTTY

Copyright © 2019 Ahamed Kutty
All rights reserved
First Edition

PAGE PUBLISHING, INC.
Conneaut Lake, PA

First originally published by Page Publishing 2019

ISBN 978-1-64544-843-3 (pbk)
ISBN 978-1-64544-844-0 (digital)

Printed in the United States of America

"To each one of you We have given a specific law (unique, different) and a pattern of life." Qur an 5:48.

Ahamed kutty M.D

Dedication

This book is dedicated, as its name indicates, to the discoverers of the double helix, James Watson and Francis Crick. The double Helix is a graphic representation of the structure of the DNA in our body.

Additionally, to the millions of individuals born with a cognitive defect or a physical abnormality due to harmful mutations either due to errors in chromosome duplication or due to exposure to harmful agents to the fetus. This book is dedicated to all would-be mothers who will listen to the health professionals' advice as to how to avoid any harmful effects to the fetus. It is the responsibility of the parents to bring to this word a child who is perfect mentally and physically and not with any defect.

Dedication of this small book also goes to the memory of the three young girls who were raped and murdered in India recently. One was a six-month-old in Madhya Pradesh, another was an eleven-year-old unidentified girl found dead due to rape on the street in Surat, Gujrat, and the unkindest, brutal murder of an eight-year-old girl in Jammu in India, and many others.

The one particular incident perpetrated against this eight-year-old girl was the most gruesome torture human beings can commit against an innocent girl. She was abducted by adults and a juvenile of a different religion and took her to a local temple where she was drugged and raped for four days in front of God's idol then her head was hit with a large stone, and finally she was strangled to death. The house of worship was turned into a house of rape, torture, and murder of an innocent Muslim girl.

Regardless of the religion of the victim, these heinous crimes have to be stopped. The torture perpetrated against this Muslim girl, Asifa Bano, is a reflection of the violent turn that genetic expression can take due to the influence of epigenetics. The society where the perpetrators lived was infused with the poison of hatred against the local Muslims by the majority community and eventually the criminals lost all sense of human dignity due to transformation of genetic expression to the heinous act of aggression due to the influence of antisocial thoughts on epigenetics.

Her memory will remain in our minds forever. I, along with over a billion Indians who could not save these innocent lives, regardless of their religious persuasion, can only ask for their forgiveness.

This incidence has shaken the conscience of the fair minded, silent majority of Indians and they have voiced their disgust and anguish against it, throughout India and their voices will prevail.

Destiny Acknowledgment

I have to express my gratitude to the following individuals for helping in compiling this book:

My wife, Mymoona Kutty and my three sons—Malik Kutty, Rafiq Kutty, and Thoufiq Kutty—in arranging the text of the book, Danielle Golden and Anna Wendlick for creating the pictures, and Miss Sehar Azad and Mike Valentino for editing. Additionally I acknowledge the efforts of Kathleen Gallagher, Samar Kutty, Layla Kutty and Kabir Kutty in preparing the index.

CHAPTER 1

Predestination/Destiny

Predestination: In religious circles, it means an individual's fate is already decreed long before he or she is conceived in the womb, and some believe even before the universe was created by the Almighty God. This concept, predestination or fate, is mentioned in all religions in one fashion or the other. It is based on the belief that Almighty God is aware of anything and everything from the beginning of the universe or even before till the end of the universe. And God can evaluate and see anything and everything that each person does or even thinks of doing in the future and create a record of his or her activities during the entire life.

This belief is based on the assumption that human beings are restricted in their vision and knowledge of events beyond the present moment. We cannot predict what will happen next moment or tomorrow. But God is beyond time and space, and He can observe and "see" what has happened from the initial creation of the universe and even before and what will happen till the end of the universe. This specifically relates to the future of a human being's soul, particularly concerning its fate. This concept has led many to believe in the futility of doing any good deeds, as he or she might have already been condemned to hell.

God can see and evaluate the sum total of a person's activities, even if he or she will be born one hundred or ten thousand years from now and make a report card, at any time, long before the person's birth. This does not mean God is making a person do bad or good deeds against the person's free will, since all the deeds are determined by his or her genetic makeup (DNA) and free will. God is only doing an evaluation of a person's life. Since God can see far into the future including the death and resurrection, where all good and bad deeds will be evaluated and judged, God is capable of making that judgment now. But the good deeds that one does will always be rewarded and that will influence God's final judgment.

Human beings can only evaluate our activities of today and the activities of the past, and from that, he or she can make some assumption of his or her potential fate. But we cannot evaluate what we will be doing in the future, which may be good and can influence God's scoreboard and judgment and therefore doing good things is always beneficial.

Whether it is good karma, as in Hindu philosophy, repentance and remedial activities as described in Abrahamic religion, all will have beneficial effects on the genetic expression because of the influence of epigenetics as described in later chapters.

Under predestination or destiny, all events have been willed by God, including our physical existence and eventually the fate of our soul. Often this brings into focus the free will of human beings and the involvement of God in our day to day life. God is knowledgeable about everything about the human being's physical and mental faculties. And God has predetermined everything pertaining to an individual before his or her birth. Everything that he or she does or even his or her thoughts and the eventual fate of the person's soul are predetermined.

But God is beyond time and space, and He can observe and "see" what has happened from the creation of the universe and till the end of the universe and all events that can happen, or that had happened to all living creatures. Of course, there have been debates as to what aspects of our life are included under the broad field of predetermination. Are good and bad deeds involved or only good deeds are predetermined and bad deeds are purely determined by the individual's actions or free will?

The Arabic word for predetermination is Al-Qadar and it is included in the traditional belief among Muslims-Al-Qada-wal Qadar (the divine decree and will), and to some it is the sixth pillar of Islamic faith. During the Umayyad dynasty from AH 41-132 (CE 661-750) they believed that everything man does is predetermined by God. But opponents argued that good deeds are from God and bad deeds were caused by human beings and further they said in that Umayyad rulers wanted to hide their bad deeds under the guise of predetermination decreed by God, and they introduced the concept of free will with predetermination (5).

Even in pre-Islamic Arabia, the pagans held a firm belief in predestination to include all aspects of life, whether poverty, illness, death, or fortunes. This is evident in the poetry written by the Arabs during that time. Some interpreted this as a mechanism to cope with adversities, as it was interpreted as an act of God and therefore people should be content with it and nothing can be done about it. Even today most believers do the same. Whether good or bad, all events will be explained on the basis of divine decree, and they find no benefit in complaining about it, as all are preordained by the Almighty. This belief gives them some mental satisfaction when faced with adverse events.

There are different meanings for the Arabic word *Qadar* (predetermination), however, depending on the circumstances and context where the word is used.

Most Arabic words have multiple meanings depending on what context it is used. Qadar means, among other things, predestination. The root of the word is Q-D-R and the meaning includes determine, decide, decree, make a thing according to its measure, ability to do, accomplish, or achieve or attain a goal or power or ability to do something. Moreover, Qadar also means to measure, to assess, and to determine.

The related word Taqdeer refers primarily to making a thing according to predefined measures, standards, or criteria (plan). Some references to Qadar and the deeds of God explain the meaning of Qadar. Quran 25:2, "He to whom belongs the dominion of heavens and earth, no son has He begotten, nor has He a partner in His dominion. He has created all things and ordered them in due proportions." The quote implies accurate planning or measure.

Quran 30:38, "And the sun: it runs its appointed course. Such is the making of things by the Almighty. The knower, according to his self-defined measures" (taqdeer).

Quran 40:57. "The creation of the heavens and earth is even more awesome than the creation of human beings, but most people do not know".

Quran 13:2, "God is the one who raised the heavens without pillars that you can see, then assumed all authority. He committed the sun and the moon, each running in its orbit for a predetermined time."

Quran 54:49. "Surely we have created everything with predetermination." (according to proportion, measure, certain purpose)

Qadar and taqdeer denote creation of something with a design, structure, and function, whether the universe, heaven, earth, or human being.

About the Creation of Man

In the Bible: Genesis 2:7 says, "Then the Lord God formed man of dust from the ground and breathed in to his nostrils the breath of life and man became a living being."

In the Quran 28:12-14, "Verily we created man from a product of wet earth, then placed him as a drop (of seed) in a safe lodging, then we fashioned the drop into a clot then we fashioned the clot into a little lump then we fashioned the little lump into bones, then clothed bones with flesh and produced it another creation. So blessed be God, the best of creators."

This is Qadar of human beings-the design (plan) stages of development (fertilization, cell division, development of organs), structure and function, and the end product being the infant.

So this plan and the execution of the plan resulting in our birth is predetermination. Whether a child is born normal or with deformity or other biochemical abnormality is also predetermined (see scientific explanation that follows). We the human beings are content with the idea that everything is predetermined by God whether good or bad and what is the point of doing good deeds and becoming good social individuals, and consequently some believe in spending life in total enjoyment and relaxation as they believe that their fate is already decided and sealed.

Can we explain this concept of predestination or "fate" on the basis of science, specifically DNA and genetics? I believe we can clearly see the correlation between what we see in our physical manifestations and events in life or mental manifestations that we ascribe to fate, and the involvement of DNA and genes. Before we embark on a brief introduction to genetics, however, we need to first look at the fundamental unit of life-" the cell"-and the amazing functions of human cells and its contents like the nucleus, chromosomes, and the DNA and also we need to look briefly at the mechanism of hereditary transmission of traits and heritable features from generation to generations.

When discussing genetics, the nineteenth-century naturalist and scientist Gregor Mendel cannot be forgotten. He was a monk in his early years and joined St. Thomas Monastery in Austria. He studied pea plants in the garden of the monastery. Here Mendel studied how the color of the plant is transmitted from parent plants to the next generation as well as how the shape of seeds (round or wrinkled) was transmitted to the newly formed plants. His studies resulted in his discovery that all these traits were transferred from parents to offspring (through units of inheritance). Which is now referred to as genes, and he also established the phenomena of dominant and recessive traits. He is called the father of genetics.

In 1859 Charles Darwin put forward the theory "evolution by natural selection." As an example of natural selection let us look at a group of short-necked and long-necked giraffes. There might have been herds of giraffes with short necks and long necks in the remote past and the long-necked ones will have a survival advantage over the short-necked ones as they can get leaves from higher trees than the short-necked ones and eventually the short-necked ones will perish due to lack of food (natural selection). This is why now we see all giraffes with long necks.

In 1953 James Watson and Francis Crick published in "Nature" the landmark study "Molecular Structure of Nucleic acid: A Structure for Deoxyribonucleic Acid". They also revealed the yet unknown design of the chromosome as a double helix. This had become a milestone in molecular biology research. Some compared its significance to the work of Gregor Mendel and Charles Darwin.

Since the discovery of the structure of DNA, molecular biology has taken a quantum jump in DNA research, and we are gifted with the human genome by later scientists. Since then, significant and fast discoveries have culminated in the human Genome project.

Human genome is a complete set of our DNA including all of its genes. The genome contains all of the information to build and maintain our body and life. In our body, a copy of the entire genome is stored in each cell that has a nucleus. We have about three billion DNA base pairs in each cell. As we can see in the later chapters, these DNA base pairs have total control of our actions, thoughts, longevity, and our performance including free will. However, full genetic expression by the DNA can be altered by epigenetics.

CHAPTER 2

Predestination in Christianity/ Destiny in Christianity

Predestination is the teaching that God has determined freely from all eternity what so ever shall come to pass (Ephesians:1:11) which says "Also we have obtained an inheritance, having been predestined according to Him who works all things after the counsel of His will." It refers to the divine determination of human beings to eternal salvation or eternal damnation. Some extend predetermination to include God having decided in advance the events of each day in an individual's life.

In the New Testament, the word *predestination* appears five times.

1. Acts 4:28, To do whatever Your hand and Your purpose predestined to occur."
2. Romans:8:29–30 "For which He foreknew He also predestined to become conformed to the image of His son."
3. First Corinthians.2:7. "but We speak God's wisdom in a mystery, the hidden wisdom which God predestined before the ages to our glory."
4. Ephesians 1:5, "He predestined us to adoption as sons through Jesus Christ to Himself."

5. Ephesians 1:11, "Also we have obtained an inheritance, having been predetermined according to His purpose who works all things after the counsel of His free will."

There are two schools of thought. One is that God has foreknowledge, that is, He knew who would choose Him and those are the ones He predestined to salvation. The other view is held by Calvinists who believe God's sovereignty, of His own free will predestined certain people to be saved and His choice is not based upon looking into the future to see who would pick Him.

Some believe that this ultimate destiny of each individual was determined before the world was created.

CHAPTER 3

Predestination/Destiny in Hinduism

In ancient India, there were some schools who believed in fatalism also known as determinism. One such sect was called the Ajivaka sect. They believed in passive living and considered all human efforts as a waste of time. One of the prominent persons of that belief was Gosala who propagated this concept.

Mahavira and Buddha, who were contemporaries of Gosala, believed in karma. Gosala believed in Niyati or determinism in which the world moved in a predetermined order and plan and each being moved in the direction of its destiny according to its chance and disposition. In the philosophy of Ajivakas, there is no place for free will.

While Hinduism does not endorse fatalism, the average Hindu believes in fate. The popular belief is that Brahma writes his fate on his forehead before he or she is born. Swami Vivekanandahas said, "Man is himself the creator of his destiny which he experiences in his life through the events."

Karma is generally defined in three ways. Activities that help spiritual evolution is called karma. That which makes him devolve spiritually is called Vikarma. Actions that help him liberate from the cycle of birth-death is called Akarma.

CHAPTER 4

Predestination/Destiny in Islam

The Arabic word for predestination is *Qadar* (destiny). *Qadha* is the word for decree, and both can be used interchangeably depending on the context in which it is used. According to the Muslim doctrine of predestination, God has spelled out the life span of every individual, their achievements, good and bad, their rewards or defaults and anything and everything including the fate of the soul even before his or her birth or even before conception.

It is customary among Muslims to address any future happenings or plans that might come along with the adage "In-shah Allah" (God willing). This is a recognition that human beings cannot foresee what will happen in the future, only God can. Qadar (predestination) is included, according to some, in the Muslim aqidah (the sixth pillar of faith), in the written document, the heavenly "tablet" kept in the heaven called "Al-Lahwu Al-mahfoos." Quran 85:22. It is also believed that anything and everything that had happened and will happen in the life of an individual in the future, is recorded on that tablet, and that will come to pass as written therein. (We will discuss the tablet later).

There were different viewpoints on Qadar (predestination) in early Islam. The Al-Jibiriya group believed that human beings have no control of events and everything will happen according to the will of God.

The Al-Qadiriyya group believed the exact opposite, that a human being's action is entirely controlled by man and God has nothing to do with it.

The Sunnis believe that God knows everything about human action, but human beings have full control of events, the free will. They also believe that Qadar (predestination) is part of Aqidha, the creed that everything will happen according to what is written on the heavenly tablet.

Quran 85:21 "this divine writ which they reject is a discourse sublime upon an imperishable tablet (inscribed) (Asad). Many commentators like Tabari, RazTi, Ibn Kathir believe that the word *tablet* is a metaphorical description for the indestructibility of the Quran and also to state that the Quran will be preserved without additions or deletions or any alteration to it. It is believed that, what is recorded in Vedas, Torah, and Injeel (Bible) may have been misrepresented or lost due to the method and timing of their writing.

This assumption is valid in that Quran was recorded or written on rocks, leaves, or animal skin and bone immediately after it was revealed to the prophet and was memorized by the companions. Today, Quran is memorized by millions of scholars called Hafiz and they recite Quran daily, from beginning to the end, without any alteration, mistakes, or loss of its textual contexts, throughout the world. This practice of recording and memorizing contemporaneously when the revelations were made makes Quran unique in protecting every divine message accurately without any omission or alteration. In the case of the Bible, Paul started writing the bible thirty years after the disappearance of Jesus.

To imagine that Quran is written "on a tablet" and kept in heaven is inconceivable as God is all knowing and omnipotent and does not need a written document (Quran) to refer to. The words inscribed on the tablet only refers to the fact Quran will never be adulterated or misrepresented as if "it is etched in stone" so to speak. Therefore, we need to explore the possibility of something else to explain what is written on the "tablet." Could it be the history of life starting from the first life form on earth 3.5 billion years ago and is inscribed in our chromosomes and DNA and the language of communication-the genetic code-that has never been altered over billions of years. Of course, there are alterations in DNA as designed by God, called mutations, but the genetic code itself is not altered over 3.5 billion years.

Let us look at the genome in our body to further explore the concept of what is written on the tablet, as it is intended for man to use for his benefit. What is written on the tablet and kept in the heaven cannot be the Quran, as mentioned above. If it is to protect against any addition, misrepresentation, or any alteration in Quran, the following points will argue against it being Quran:

1. There are adequate mechanisms against tampering with the Quran on earth, namely the availability of the old and original handwritten copies of Quran, in various centers of Islamic studies, the billions of copies of Quran that are in the possession of Muslims worldwide, and the millions of Hafils (Hafiz) who can memorize the Quran in full, throughout the world. It is to be kept in mind that the majority of Muslims do not understand the Arabic language to detect any alterations in Quran, but there are other sources to ward of any tampering as described above.
2. God does not communicate with human beings other than through prophets. Any correction that were done in the previously revealed books like the Torah and Injeel (bible) were done through successive prophets. According to our faith, Prophet Muhammad is the last prophet for our race (Adamic race) till Qiyama (end of the world), and prophet Muhammad has come and gone and there is no chance to do any correction; if for argument's sake, had any tampering with Quran ever occurred, as there is no other prophet to come and correct it, during the span of the human species, as Prophet Muhammad is the last prophet.

As revealed in Quran 61:6, Jesus says, "O children of Israel! Behold I am an apostle of God unto you (sent) to confirm the truth of whatever still remains of the Torah and to give you glad tidings of an apostle who shall come after me, whose name shall be Ahmed."

This correction of Torah was through Jesus, and as revealed in Quran 5:48, "And unto thee O prophet have We vouchsafed this divine writ, setting forth the truth, confirming the truth of whatever there still remains of earlier revelations and determining what is true therein. Judge, then, between the followers of earlier revelation in accordance with what God has bestowed from on high and do not follow their errant views."

Here it was through Prophet Muhammad the correction of previous revelation, Injeel (Bible), was done. Therefore, a heavenly correction for any alteration in Quran cannot occur as no prophet will come to us as Prophet Muhammad is the last prophet. And the description of "inscribed on the tablet" must be a metaphorical description to suggest that Quran is unalterable. This does not mean that Quran is written on the Tablet.

Or as mentioned in Quran 4:133 "If He so Wills, He can cause you Mankind to disappear, and bring forth other beings (in your stead) for God has indeed power to do this." In this scenario there could be a new prophet for this "new race" and a "new book" for their guidance and in that scenario correction of any alterations or deletions in Quran can be expected as we have seen for previous revelations. Even if alteration in the earthly copy of Quran has occurred, God can correct it through a new prophet and God will not need to refer to the inscriptions on the so-called tablet for the missing information as He is all knowing (we believe that Quran will remain inviolable). But only God knows what is in His mind.

The Heavenly Tablet

Heavenly book: The Bible refers to several heavenly books, the book of life and the book of deeds. (In the Bible: Luke:10:20, Exodus 32:32, Psalms:69:28, Daniel: 12:1).

These will be used, according to the Bible, during eschatology for judgment or, as Muslims call it, the Qiyama and resurrection and final judgment.

With respect to the heavenly tablet, even before the biblical account, it is mentioned in the Sumerian document. The Sumerian Goddess Nungal possessed "a tablet of life" in a hymn to the God Haia, where we read: "Grant to Prince Rim-Sin a reign all joyous and length of days! On a tablet of life never to be altered, place its (the reign's) name."

There is a text from the time of the Neo-Assyrian emperor Esarhaddon (680-169 B.C) that mentions a heavenly book.

In Quran, there is one reference to the tablet in Sura 85:22 where the divine writ is inscribed on it. But there are references to other divine records of God's decree suggesting there could be multiple books, tablets, or other recording devices, for God to record Eg: Quran: 22:70: Did you know that God knows (all) that is in the heavens and the earth? It is (all) in a record. Surely that is easy for God.

Quran: 35:11 "And ageth not any aged nor is reduced from anyone's life, but it is all in a book. Verily it is easy for God.

This book or record referring to aging and death clearly refers to the Telomere in our chromosome that determines our life span.

The question then, is, does God need a record or a book like we human beings use, to refer and refresh the revelations?

Quran 2:2, 106: 13:39 describes God as the source of all revelations. None of them says it was reproduced from a heavenly tablet, or a book or a slate.

Let us look at other Suras referring to the records of decree.

Quran 35:11 "And (remember) God created (every one of you) out of dust, then out of a drop of sperm and then He fashioned you into either of the sexes. And no female conceives or gives birth unless it be with His knowledge, and none that is long lived has his days lengthened and neither is aught lessened of his days-unless it be thus laid down in God's decree, for, behold it is easy for God."

Here God's decree refers to the longevity of an individual. Some people die old, others at a young age, unless an accident or natural disaster strikes, then all involved will die at the same time. This variation in death due to natural causes is decreed by God in the health of the telomere in our chromosome as described under telomere. This is not a decree from a heavenly tablet.

Quran 33:6 says that the prophet has a higher claim on believers than they have on their own selves, seeing that he is a father to them and his wives are their mothers and they who are thus closely related have, in accordance with God's "decree," a higher claim upon one another than was even the case between the believers of Yathrib and those who had migrated there for the sake of God. Nonetheless, you have to act with utmost goodness toward your close friends as well. This too is written down in God's decree. This statement refers to the injunctions that are conveyed in Quran as to how we should behave to our compatriots. This does not suggest that it comes from a heavenly tablet.

Quran 57:22, "No calamity can ever befall the earth, and neither your own selves, unless it be laid down in Our 'decree' before We bring it into being verily, all this is easy for God."

The phrase that no calamity can ever befall the earth unless it be laid down in our "decree" is a reference to the laws of nature. The Big Bang, the dusty aftermath, evolution of sun, moon, earth, and stars, the gravitational pull, and the earth's path of orbit, all with precision and without any faults, were decreed per the law of nature established by Him. We do not know if this law of nature is recorded on any heavenly tablet or not. But there is no mention of it.

The second part of this verse that reads "and neither your own selves" must refer to personal catastrophes that afflict human beings physically and not spiritually. If it is a spiritual catastrophe, then it must dwell in the decrees or instructions given in the Quran by God. But if the catastrophe is physical, then it must be "decreed" somewhere other than the Quran as there is no reference to physical catastrophe happening to human beings if certain instructions in the Quran are violated. Therefore with regards to the physical catastrophe, where will be the source of the statement "unless it be laid down in Our decree before We bring it in to being". Since it is not Quran, where is this decree regarding the catastrophe kept?

The answer is the human genome!

The physical catastrophe (devastating illness) could be a heart attack (myocardial infarction) or a stroke (paralysis) both of which can have tremendous impact on the life of an individual. These maladies afflict the individual suddenly at any time, any day, but actually the underlying pathology of these ailments, the narrowing of the blood vessels that go to the heart or the brain starts slowly over months or years and suddenly when the lumen of the blood vessel is too small, blood flow stops, and heart attack or stroke happens. There are many causes for this blood vessel narrowing and one can control most of these causative agents, like hypertension, diabetes, smoking, alcohol use, and sedentary lifestyle. But one very important cause is the genetic factor and that is in our genome. In human beings, our actions, behavior, thoughts, and achievements are controlled by the DNA and genes and therefore one can argue that our fate, predestination, or Al-Qadar (Arabic for fate) are directed and controlled by DNA and genes.

As mentioned in the beginning of this chapter, the Akkadian, the Sumerian documents, the Hebrew Bible, and the Bible all refer to the heavenly book of life. At that time, science was not developed and was ignorant about the function of our body, leave alone the knowledge about DNA and genes. This "book of life" probably is a reference to the intricate working of our genome-DNA and genes that are the sole elements in the body that maintain and propagate our life, influencing our thoughts and actions. The human being has a soul and a physical structure called the body. Religious books like Quran, Bible, and Torah primarily teach us how to keep the soul pure and god loving and the DNA and genes keep the physical body functional. The nature of the soul (or Ruh in Islamic faith) is not known to human beings, except it does not need food or clothing, and it does not die.

Some biblical writings (Jehovah's witness.org) suggest soul refers to human beings and animals and spirit refers to life.

In Islam, Soul and Ruh are used interchangeably and says no one other than God knows what the soul/Ruh is. In Quran 39:42, sleep is described as a process very close to death. If we analyze sleep, one can assume that the RUH is a variant of reticular activating system. When we sleep, we are totally unaware of our surroundings (loss of awareness), but all our vital functions of the body are working without interruption. This means that life is preserved but awareness is lost. But when we touch the sleeping person or make a loud noise, the person wakes up and he or she becomes fully awake and become aware of everything. The reticular activating system becomes active and is back to normal and functioning.

Quran further states that those who are destined to die, the RUH/soul, will not come back, but to those who are not destined to die, the RUH/soul returns. Therefore the RAS (reticular activating system) can be called the RUH/soul at death the RAS dies as well. But the RUH is taken away by the angel of death to be stored till the day of judgement. The information contained in the RAS is carried to the storage place in the form of RUH. The nature of RUH is unknown to man yet.

We have referred to the heavenly books, the book of life and the book of decrees and deeds. But the so called books may not be books at all. When these divine revelations like Torah, Bible (Injeel), or Quran were revealed the only place where information was stored, was a book. At that time whether it is population register, business transactions, trade information, for buying and selling, etc, were all recorded in the form of books. And consequently when God refers to information and divine writ stored in heaven, God has to use the word *book* for us to comprehend. But now we have come a long way from the past and our information storage capacity has grown leaps and bounds, like the tiny computer chip from Silicon Valley, where trillions of files can be stored. The so called heavenly books may all be the ultimate source of knowledge and information-the almighty God.

As mentioned earlier the Al-Lahw Al-Mahfuz (the Tablet) means a flat bone, white bone or flat surface or flat wood or anything written on. If it is meant to be the bone it suggests that the inscription or writings on it refers to the DNA and the genetic code and the DNA alphabets–the book of life. The DNA can be extracted from the bone millions of years after the animal or man dies. DNA is unique for each individual like the finger print. The entire formula for human life and death is inscribed in the genetic code. Al-Lahw if it refers to the bone it suggests the ability of bone to preserve the inscribed information–the genetic code our book of life–without loss for millions of years. Quran is not a book of life rather it is a book that teaches human beings how to live one's life.

All religions are designed for spiritual enhancement of mankind and to emancipate our soul. In Hinduism, the major impact on salvation is karma. In Judaism, God has given Ten Commandments to follow. The religion of Islam is based on five fundamental creeds:

1. Believe in God and His messenger—Muhammad is the messenger.
2. Prayer five times.
3. Fasting in the month of Ramzan.
4. Pay Zakath—a percentage of wealth for social services.
5. Hajj—pilgrimage to Mecca.

Strangely enough our body, which houses the soul, is created out of five bases:

1. Adenine
2. Cytosine
3. Guanine
4. Thymine
5. Uracil

CHAPTER 5

Epigenetics

Epigenetics is the study of heritable changes in gene expression (active versus inactive genes) that do not involve changes to the underlying DNA sequence—a change in phenotype without change in genotype—which in turn affect how cells read the genes. In other words, how genes are switched on and off. Epigenetic change is a regular and natural occurrence but can also be influenced by several factors including age, the environment, lifestyle, food, smoking behavior, physical activity, working habits, alcohol, and stress—all will have either positive or negative impacts on gene expression through epigenetics.

"Epi" means over and above the DNA. Epigenetics control DNA. At least three systems including DNA methylation, histone modification, and noncoding RNA associated gene silencing are currently considered to initiate and sustain epigenetic change.

Epigenetic diseases: cancer, mental retardation disorders, neuropsychiatric disorders, and several pediatric syndromes.

Einstein, Tesla, and the science of quantum physics have shown that the fabric of the universe is composed of vibrational strings expressed as energy. Every single cell and organ system, as well as our body, is surrounded by its own individual energy field. Our very life is a reflection of our own vibrational essence. Since the discovery of the nature of DNA by James Watson and Francis Crick in 1953, it is believed that genes control biology and later this concept evolved into the belief of genetic determinism, the notion that our physical and behavioral fates are encoded in the genes.

Research by cellular biologist Bruce Lipton shows that our genes and DNA are activated and influenced by signals from outside the cell membrane. That influence over and above the DNA is called the epigenetics. The American space agency NASA reported on March 16th 2018, the changes in genetic expression that happened in a twin brother who lived in space for one year. The other brother remained on earth. NASA scientists discovered that the astronaut had evidence of changes in gene expression during space travel that gradually returned back to prespace condition in 97% of the genes. This further confirms the fact that external factors in this case space travel can bring about changes in gene expression-Epigenetics.

CHAPTER 6

The Cell

In order to unravel the mystery involved in the commonly used term *predestination*, one needs to study the source of previously hidden but now revealing secrets of our life—the human cell. Let us see what is hidden inside the tiny human cell. A cell is defined as the basic unit or building block of all living things except viruses. How many cells are there in our body is not clear. A rough estimate is that there are thirty to forty trillion cells in our body. The cells provide the structure and function of the body including life. They take in nutrients from food and convert into energy for our body's functions. The cell contains different ingredients, including the nucleus, which contains the genetic material or DNA.

The cell is a microscopic structure and cannot be seen with the naked eye. The cell was discovered by Robert Hooke in 1665 and the name cell was coined due to their similarity to cells inhabited by Christian monks in the monastery.

The cell theory was developed by Matthias Jacob Schneider and Theodor Schwab in 1839 and states that all living things are composed of one or more cells, and they are the fundamental units of structure and function of all living organisms. Each cell comes from preexisting cells, and they contain genetic information to be transmitted to the next generation.

It is believed that the first living cell appeared on earth about 3.5 billion years ago.

CHAPTER 7

The Human Cell

Early biologists thought that the cell is a sac containing some fluid and certain floating debris. But today's biologists know that the cell is the fundamental unit for our survival, our life, thoughts, and growth and reproduction. We need to explore what is inside this magical bullet "the cell" that is so essential for our life. (See picture.)

The Human Cell

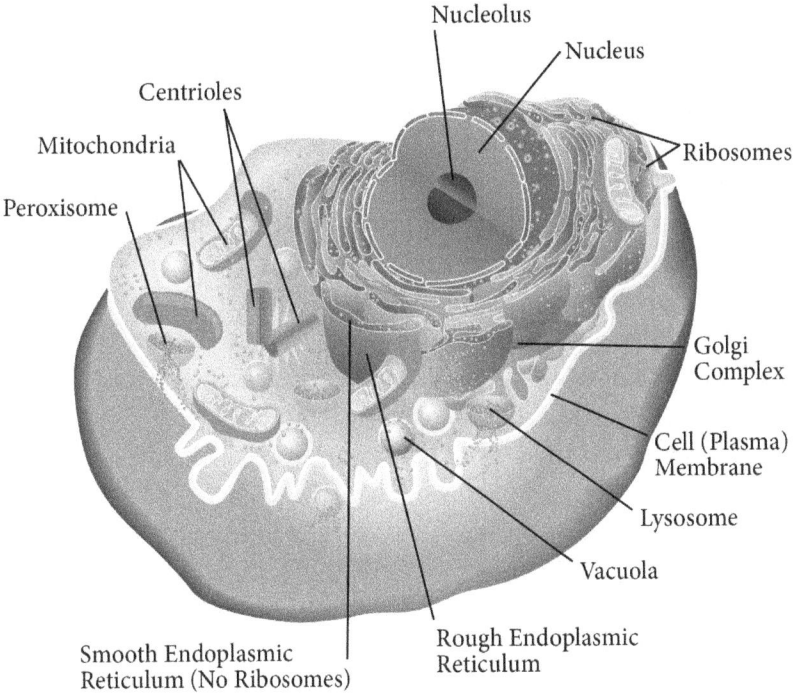

Fig. 1

When exploring the structure of the cell, first we see the outer covering called the cell membrane. It is made of a double phospholipids membrane, which has selective permeability, in which it allows the nutrients and oxygen in and waste products of metabolism that takes place in the cell out. It separates internal metabolic events from the external environment of the cell.

When one visualizes the interior of the cell, first we encounter a gel-like material called the cytoplasm, which consists of 90 percent water; the rest is salts, organic molecules, and many enzymes, proteins, and nutrients. The cytoplasm plays an important role in the cell where in it holds the suspended organelles. It helps to maintain the shape of the cell and its consistency, and stores chemicals for metabolism.

The cytoskeleton is made of proteins in the form of tiny threads. It helps cells to maintain their shape. It has three components: microtubules, actins filaments and intermediate fibers.

Organelles are the small "factories" where all the metabolic activities are performed in the cell. Each organelle produces a specific product that is used in the cell or in the body.

The nucleus: Cells of living organisms are divided into two kinds. One is the prokaryocytes, like the bacteria which has no nucleus, and the other is called eukaryocytes, like plants and animals that does have a nucleus. The nucleus is the largest organelle inside the cell covered by a nuclear membrane. It contains the genetic material, which is the most important structure in our body for metabolic function and reproduction.

Chromosomes: In the nucleus is the chromosomes made of chromatin and DNA. It is shaped like a double helix or ladder. This shape is seen only during cell division. 3-D X-ray diffraction pictures of the structure of DNA show different shapes as clumps of twisted material in the DNA.

Mitochondria: This organelle is called the powerhouse, which generates the ATP, which is the universal energy source for all cells. They are small sac-like structures found near the nucleus. They have their own DNA different from the DNA of the nucleus.

Endoplasmic reticulum are three dimentional flat sheets engaged in transporting cellular products and producing proteins. They are found close to the nucleus.

Golgi Apparatus packs cellular products in sacs and help transport across cell membrane.

Vacuoles carries products to cell membrane for transport.

ATP is the energy source that all cells use. The total ATP at any given time is 0.1 mole. The body needs 200–300 moles of ATP daily. The body synthesizes 200–300 moles daily. ATP cannot be stored and hence it has to be synthesized. Per hour 1 kg ATP is created in the body. A single cell uses about 10 million ATP molecules per second.

Genetic code: The genetic code is the set of rules by which information is encoded in the DNA. The mRNA sequences is communicated to the organelles to produce a specific protein by living cells. The ribosome links the amino acids in a specific order as instructed by the mRna using transfer RNA. The genetic code is similar in all organisms and can be expressed in a simple table with sixty-four characters.

In 1961, Sydney Brenner, Leslie Barnett, and R.J. Watts demonstrated that the genetic code is made up of a series of three base pairs called the codon, which codes for individual amino acids. The scientists also realized that there are sixty-four possible triplet codones since there are four nitrogenous bases ($4 \times 4 \times 4 = 64$).

DNA Double Helix

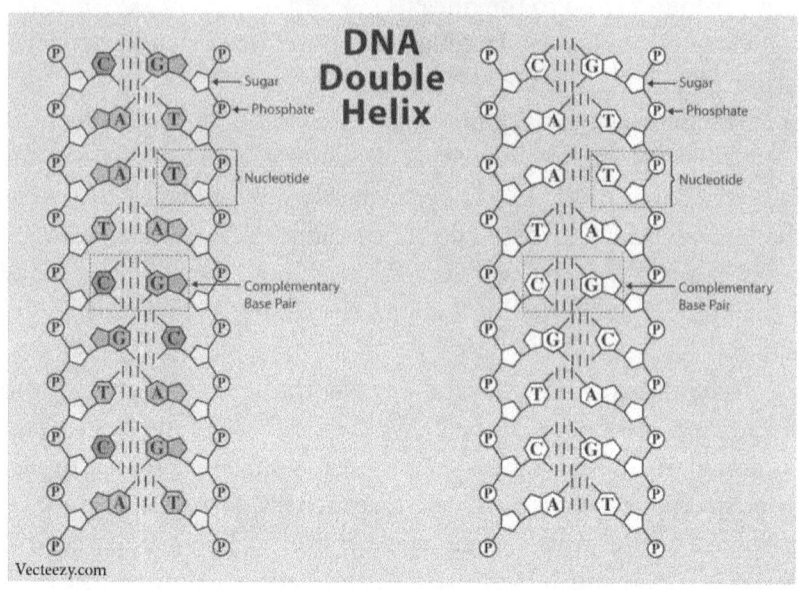

Standard Genetic Code

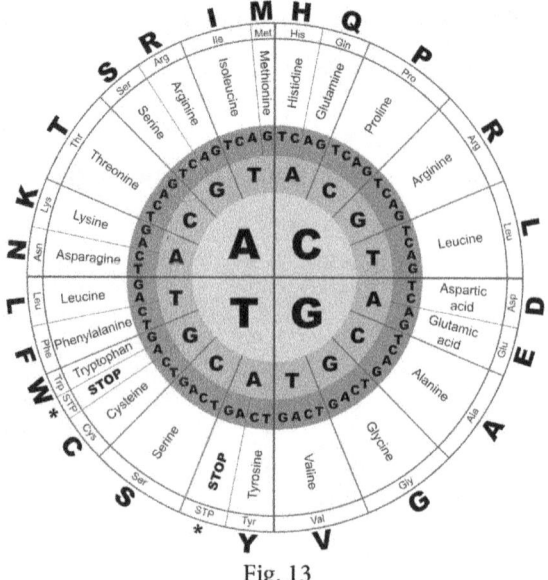

Fig. 13

Today, scientists have decoded what all these sixty-four codons encode for, and the conclusions are universal.

The genetic code is based on the sequence of the nucleotides in the gene. The mechanism of transmission of this code to the ribosomes in the cell to manufacture amino acids is elaborate and with negligible mistakes.

This communication is not based on letters or words as we use today. A successful method of communication without alphabets is the Morse code that is based on dots, dashes and spaces. Genetic code is based on the sequence of nucleotides in the gene and the method of transmission are based on biochemical principles. This unique method of communication has remained unaltered since the first unicellular organism appeared on earth 3.5 billion years ago.

CHAPTER 8

The Specialized Cell

In the human body, there are specialized cells with different function. Some of these specialized cells join together to form tissues and the tissues become specialized organs. But the basic structural organization and metabolic needs such as conversion of carbohydrates into high energy ATP and genes involving production of protein are done like any other cells.

These special organs are the brain, thyroid gland, heart, lungs, intestines, pancreas, liver, kidney, uterus, testicles, ovaries, pituitary gland, and parathyroid gland.

The specialized cells are nerve cells, epithelial cells, exocrine cells, endocrine cells, blood cells, etc.

All cells carry the same genome, but these specialized cells need to make special proteins for these different organs to function. These cells produce special proteins to fit the function of the specialized cells due to the function of the regulatory genes found in the noncoding gene population.

CHAPTER 9

Embryology

To understand our fate, we need to explore the fertilization of the ovum by the sperm and the development of the zygote. The fertilization takes place in the fallopian tube. The description of fetal development (embryology) in Quran has been a curiosity in the scientific community. Quran 39:6 "He makes you in the womb of your mother in stages, one after the other, in three veils of darkness."

In the seventh century AD, physicians were aware of the fact that the human embryo developed in the uterus. Many believe that it was unlikely they knew that the fetus developed in stages. The first illustration of a fetus in the uterus was drawn by Leonardo da Vinci in the fifteenth century. In the second century AD, Galen described in his book "on the formation of the fetus" the placenta and fetal membranes. In the fourth century B.C. Aristotle described the stages of development of chick embryo. Until the fifteenth century, however, the stages of development of human fetus was not known or discussed

It was in the seventeenth century that the microscope was discovered by Leeuwenhoek, and it was only after that the description of early stages of chick embryo were made. The description of the stages of human embryo was made in the twentieth century. (Streeter 1941, O'Rahilly 1972)

Pertaining to fetal development, Quran 39:6 says, "He creates you in the womb of your mother in stages one after the other in three veils of darkness"; Quran 23:13 "Then We placed him as a drop in a place of rest firmly fixed." The word *drop* in this context refers to the Arabic word "nuftah."

From the above, Quranic word *nufta,* from its translation, we understand that this drop or mixed cell should be the zygote, not the sperm or seminal fluid. In the fallopian tube, due to ciliary action, no cell, either sperm or ovum, can rest. The sperm and ovum are called gametes. The zygote gets embedded in the endometrium of the uterus

From the formation of the zygote, the parental genetic materials are incorporated into the growing embryo as it becomes a new individual. This new individual is already entering the world with all the preprogrammed and predetermined genetic code—the code of life called the DNA. This genetic information is stored in the DNA of the parents and a new life always begets from a previous life, the parents. Even each cell is formed from a preexisting cell. If we take the history of life, it goes back to 3.5 billion years ago when the first live unicellular organism appeared on earth. Since then, the genetic code is transmitted to the offspring through different life forms, including human beings. Therefore, life as we see it on earth today is already 3.5 billion years old after life first appeared in the unicellular life form.

The Human Ovum
(The Female Gamete)

Fertilization

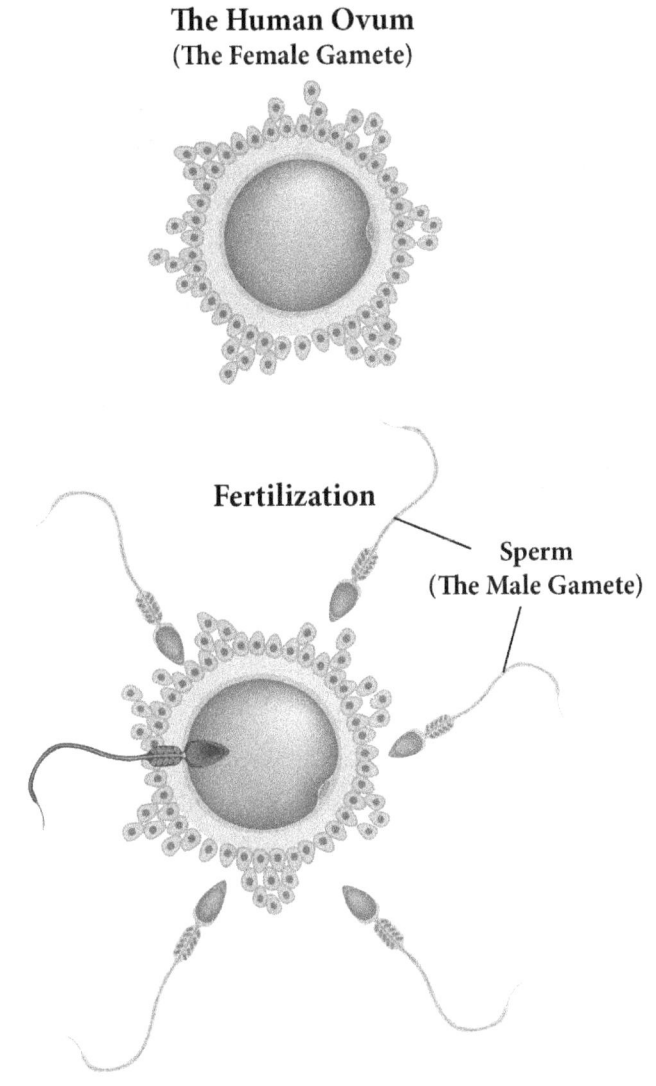

Sperm
(The Male Gamete)

During fertilization after the first sperm enters the ovum, the covering of the ovum stiffens and prevents entry of another sperm.

Fig. 5

Fertilization

The fertilization takes place in the Fallopian tube. The 23 chromosomes from the mother and 23 chromosomes from the father are joined to have 46 chromosomes. This process equips the embryo with the full complement of the chromosomes and it becomes capable of growth and development, physically, mentally and sexually, and lays the foundation for his or her destiny.

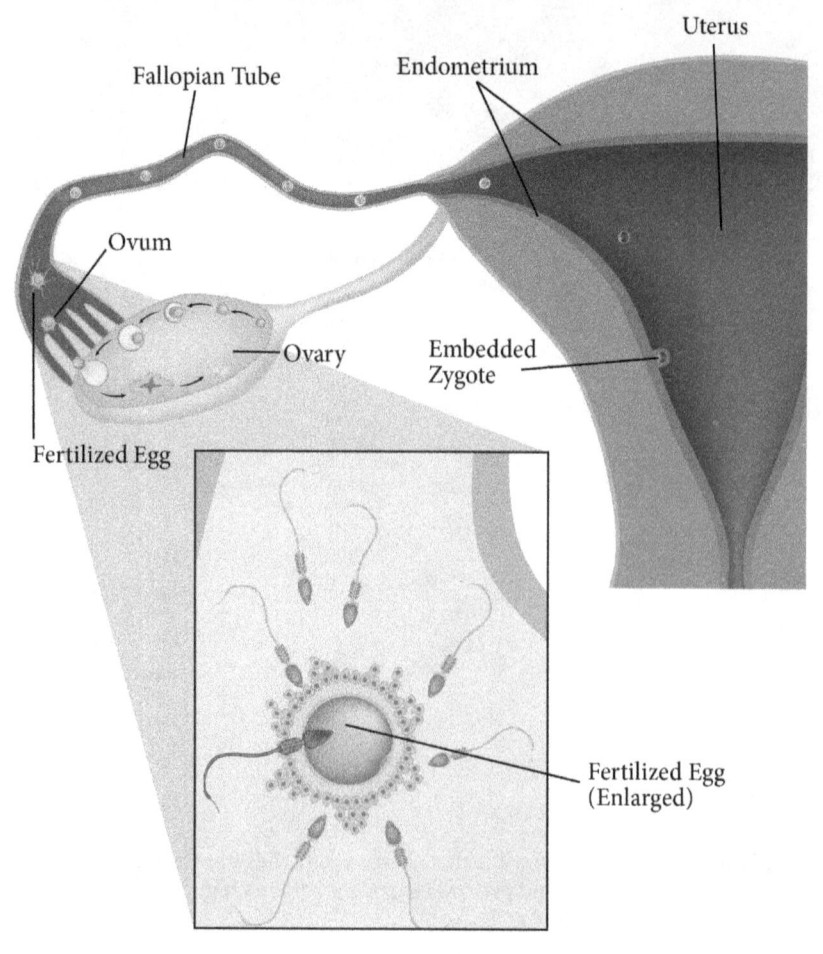

Fig. 6

Therefore, the belief in predetermination, namely all our actions and thoughts, are already inscribed in our body system through the chromosomes that house the DNA has scientific backing.

By expanding this concept, the belief that our actions and thoughts, or anything and everything we do, could have been programmed by the infinite wisdom of God even before the universe was created, as some believe, but from a practical standpoint starting with the unicellular organism 3.5 billion years ago, on earth. We see this preprogrammed transmission of genetic information over the past 3.5 billion years, which is long before human beings appeared on earth.

In human evolution, we see the emergence of Homo sapiens about two hundred thousand years ago evolved from archaic humans. Studies of fossils, cave paintings, and genomic studies suggest that modern behavior, abstract thinking, deep planning symbolic behavior like arts, music, exploitation of large game, and tool technology, etc., would have developed about fifty thousand years ago. About twelve to fifteen thousand years ago, the Adamic people appeared based on religious texts and archeological findings of cultivation and domestication of animals. This new arrival, the Adamic people, must have come from the previous generation of human species-the Cro–Magnons–the pre–Adamic people. The Cro–magnons were hunter gatherers and did not have a settled life. It was the Adamic people who started a settled life and domestication of animals according to religious books and archeology. Since the appearance of the first unicellular organism, there have been additions to genetic content due to mutation. But the fundamental principle of cell division and transmission of parental traits remains the same. One can still contend with the belief that preordainment of our life events through DNA long before our birth has valid scientific backing as the DNA and genetic code have been inscribed in our chromosomes for centuries. Additionally, our longevity and death are also inscribed in our chromosomes, through the telomere, and this is also ordained or inscribed before our birth or even before conception through the chromosomes of our parents. Our modern behavior, the hallmark of being a human, is seen in the previous generations of anatomically modern humans as far back as fifty thousand years ago.

Our genome contains information relating to previous species and maybe information relating to future novel species by way of mutations. The possibility of our race being transformed to another species is referenced in Quran.

Quran 4:133 "If He so wills He can cause you O mankind, to disappear and bring forth other beings (in your stead) for God has indeed the power to do this."

Life has continued uninterruptedly over the past 3.5 billion years since the first unicellular organism appeared on earth. Some species have disappeared, but life never came to a standstill. Life travelled through various species and now it is manifest in the human beings. Life never dies due to the mechanism of reproduction, but species die. When a child is born, he or she is not coming with a new life but is only a new life form.

CHAPTER 10

Chromosomes

Chromosomes are threadlike structures located inside the nucleus of plant or animal cells. Each chromosome is made of protein and a single molecule of deoxyribonucleic acid (DNA). The chromosome is passed from the parents to offspring, DNA contains the specific instructions that make each type of living creature unique.

The term *chromosome* comes from the Greek words for color (chromo) and body (soma). Scientists gave this name to the chromosomes because they are cell structures or bodies that are strongly stained by some colorful dyes used in research.

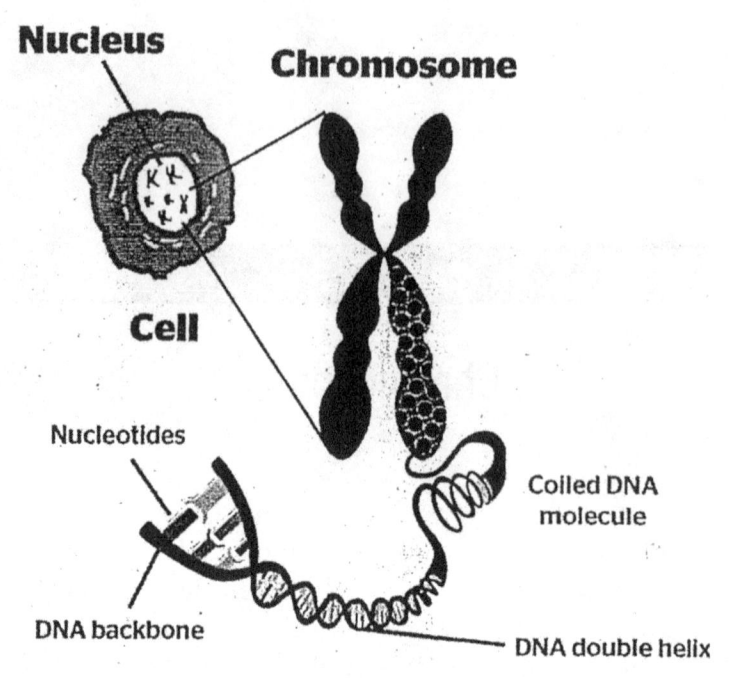

Fig 2.

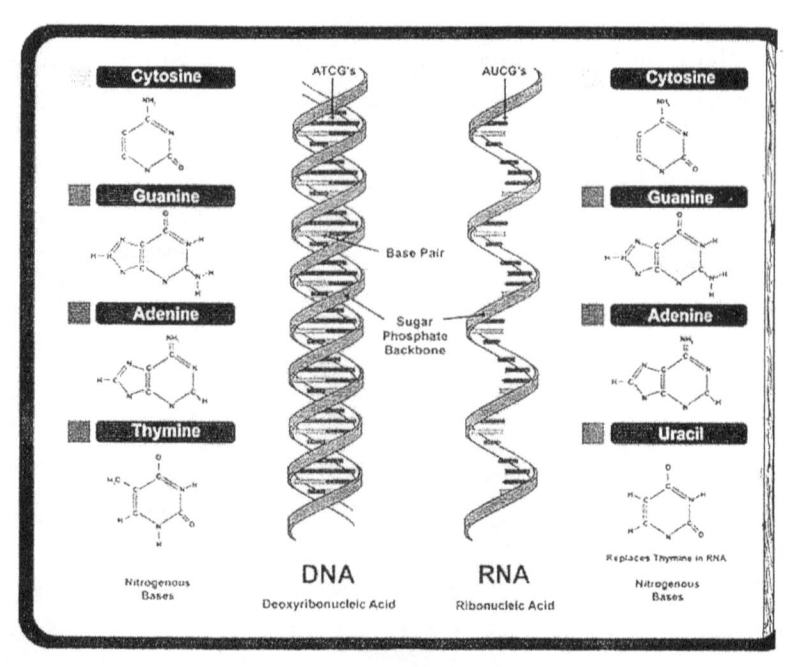

Fig. 4

44

Function of Chromosomes

The structure of chromosomes keeps DNA tightly wrapped around spool-like proteins called histones. Without such packaging, DNA molecules would be too long to fit inside cells. For example, if all the DNA molecules in a single human cell were unwound from the histones and placed end to end, they would stretch six feet!

Genes

Genes are made up of DNA. Each chromosome contains many genes.

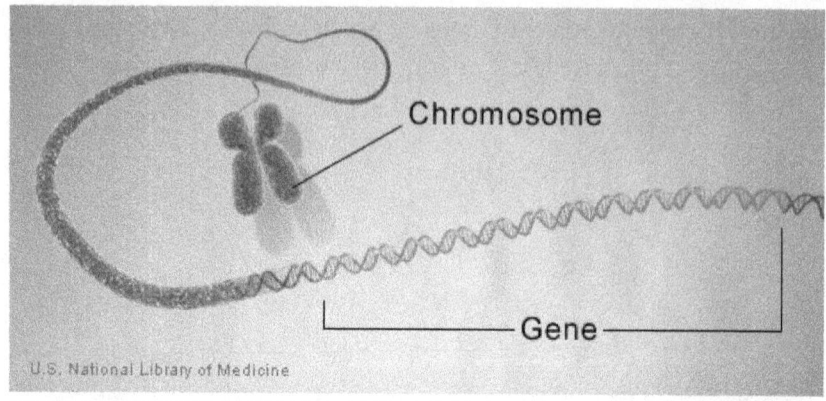

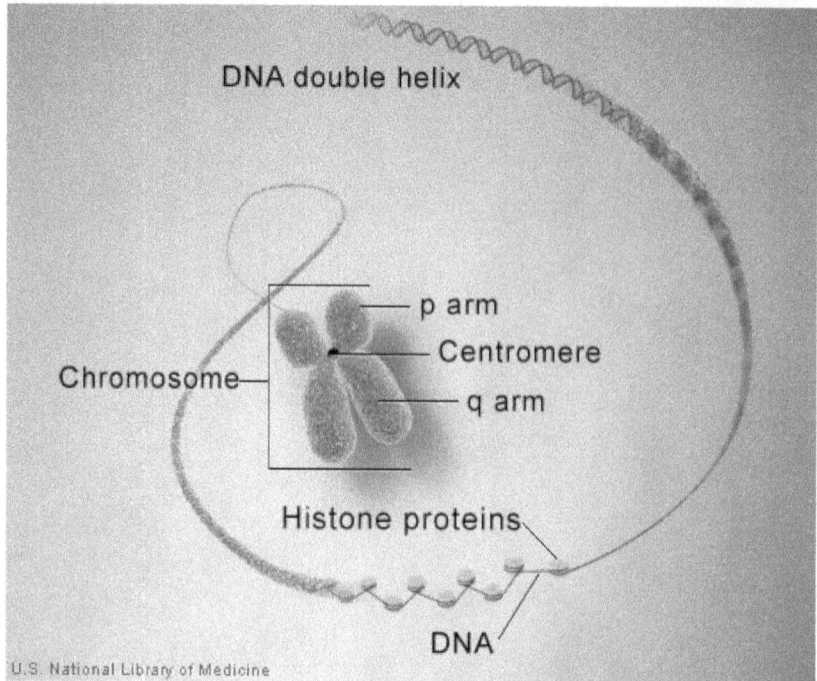

Fig. 3

THE DOUBLE HELIX-DNA

For an organism to grow and function properly, cells must constantly divide to produce new cells to replace old, worn out cells. During cell division, it is essential that DNA remain intact and evenly distributed among daughter cells. Chromosomes are a key part of this process that ensures DNA is correctly copied and distributed in the vast majority of cell divisions. Still, on rare occasions, mistakes can happen. Changes in the number or structure of chromosomes in new cells may lead to serious problems. For example, in humans, one type of leukemia and some other cancers are caused by defective chromosomes made up of joined pieces of broken chromosomes.

It is also crucial that reproductive cells, such as eggs and sperm, contain the right number of chromosomes and that those chromosomes have the correct structure. If not, the resulting offspring may fail to develop properly. For example, people with Down's syndrome have three copies of chromosome 21, instead of the two copies found in normal people.

Chromosome vary in number and shape among living things. Most bacteria have one or two circular chromosomes. Humans and plants have linear chromosomes that are arranged in pairs within the nucleus of the cell. Reproductive cells, gametes, contain only one copy of each chromosome. When male and female gametes meet, they become a single cell and will have two copies of each chromosome.

The mitochondria of human cell contains a circular chromosome. The constricted area of the chromosome is called the centromere.

It is believed that longevity is tied to genetic factors in 30 percent and the rest is due to lifestyle. The Seventh-Day Adventists in the United States live five to eight years longer than the rest of Americans, and it is believed due to their lifestyle in that they exercise, eat a vegetarian diet, and do not partake in smoking or alcohol use. It is believed that over two hundred beneficial genetic alleles influence longevity. The important ones are the FOXO3A, IGFR-I, CETP variant, SRT1, TPS3, APOC3, AKT1, and IL6.

When discussing heredity and transfer of traits from parent to offspring, one cannot forget the "father of genetics," Gregor Mendel.

Mendel was born in 1822 in Brno in the old Austrian empire. He was a monk and conducted experiments with pea plants in breeding and established many of the rules of heredity, now called the Mendelian laws of inheritance. Mendel worked with seven characteristics of the pea plant namely plant height, pod shape and color, seed shape and color, and flower position and color. Mendel published his findings in the paper "experiments on plant hybrids," but this significant scientific discovery was largely ignored by the then existing scientific community until 1900 when Mendel's discovery was reinvented and accepted as the basis for hereditary transfer of traits to offspring. Mendel also established the concept of dominant and recessive traits by his pea experiments.

Even though Mendel laid the foundation of genetics, the exact material that carry the genetic material to the offspring were not clearly identified. Initially, scientists thought that the proteins were the genetic carrier and DNA being a simple chemical, it would be impossible for DNA to carry this information. DNA contains only four different nucleotides. Proteins on the other hand contains twenty amino acids and more complex than DNA. In the 1940s, most scientists thought that the genetic information was encoded by strings of amino acids. It was clear that histones were not the genetic material as histones were not present in sperms. But sperms carry small amounts of protamines.

Discovery of the Genetic Material

By 1930, scientists knew the existence of discrete genetic material and initially thought it was the chromosome. They were not clear what kind of molecule carried the genetic information. At that time, it was known that chromosomes contained both DNA and histones.

Most people could not believe that it was possible for DNA, which contains only four nucleotides to carry the complex genetic information.

In 1928, Fred Griffin performed experiments with Streptococcus Pneumoniae that causes pneumonia. He took two strains of the bacteria, the S-strain, the virulent variety, and R-strain, the avirulent variety. He injected mice with these bacteria and found that the virulent variety will kill the mouse and the avirulent (R) strain would not. The S-strain, when grown in a petri dish, will form smooth glistening colonies due to a polysaccharide outer coating. This polysaccharide coating protects the bacteria from the host's immune system, and they become more virulent than the R variety. The R-strain, the avirulent variety, does not have the gelatinous coat outside the bacteria and the colonies look rough.

Griffith injected a mouse with S-strain and the mouse dies. A mouse injected with R-strain survived. Then he injected a mouse with heat killed S-strain and the mouse survived. Then he injected live R-strain, which normally won't kill the mouse plus heat killed S-strain, and the mouse died. This suggested to Griffith that something in the heat killed S. Strain was picked up by the R-strain and became virulent, and this was called the transforming factor.

In 1944, Oswald Avery, Colin McLeod, and Maclyn Mcarty showed that the transforming principle was the DNA. But this was not enough to convince everybody in the scientific community.

In 1952, Alfred Hershey and Martha Chase did an experiment with bacteriophage called T2. It contains only DNA and proteins. After entering a cell T2 genome directed the host cell to make new phage. Hershey and Chase grew two cultures of T2. One culture was made in the presence of radioactive phosphorus (32P), which labels newly synthesized nucleic acids and the other culture was in the presence of radioactive sulfur (35S), which preferably labels proteins.

The radio labeled phage is allowed to infect the bacterial culture growing without any radio labeled agents. Following the attachment of the phage, the culture is centrifuged and the supernatant fluid and the cells were separated and found that the DNA contained the radioactive phosphate in the cells. The supernatant fluid showed proteins and radioactive sulfur. This confirmed that the genetic material is the DNA.

CHAPTER 11

The Human Genome

The human genome is the genome of Homo sapiens. It has about three billion base pairs packed into twenty-three pairs of chromosomes in each cell in our body. A genome is an organism's complete set of DNA, including all of its genes. Each genome contains all of the information needed to build and maintain that organism. In humans, a copy of the entire genome—more than three billion DNA base pairs—is in all cells that have a nucleus. Each cell contains twenty-three pairs of chromosomes of which twenty-two pairs are called autosomal chromosomes and one pair is called sex chromosomes. Chromosomes 1–22 are numbered according to decreasing sizes.

Somatic cells have one copy of chromosomes 1–22 from each parent and an X chromosome from the mother and an X or Y chromosome from the father. There are about twenty thousand protein coding genes in the genome. Less than 2 percent of the human genome is protein coding and 98 percent are called the noncoding sequences. Many of these noncoding DNA are responsible to maintain the structure of the chromosomes and regulating the structural features of the telomere and centromeres. There are about thirteen thousand inactive copies of protein-coding genes, which are called pseudogenes. There are many regulatory sequences in the noncoding genes, which are necessary for gene expression.

THE DOUBLE HELIX-DNA

The chromosome and the DNA are cramped into the tiny nucleus of the cell. Each cell contains approximately two meters of DNA if stretched end to end, and it is housed in the nucleus, which is only about six micro m in diameter. This is equivalent to packing 40 km of fine thread into a tennis ball. This special packing is accomplished by proteins that bind to and fold DNA into a series of coils and make the DNA from untangling. Even if the DNA is tightly folded, its folding pattern enables them to be easily untangled and replicated when enzymes are added.

There are 37.2 trillion cells in a human body on the average. The human genome that has over three billion nucleotides that are distributed in twenty-three pairs of chromosomes. The DNA and the protein complex is called the chromatin. A gene is defined as a segment of DNA that contains instructions for coding for protein.

What will be the total length of DNA in the body of an adult human being? If all the tiny twisted filaments, the chromosomes, carrying the DNA are stretched and connected end to end it will traverse a distance of going from earth to the sun and back seventy times.

The distance from earth to the sun is 93,000,000 miles.

(length of base pair) (number of base pairs per cell) (number of cells in the body)

$(0.34 \times 10\text{-}9m) (6 \times 10) (10^{13})$

$= 2 \times 10 + 13$ meters = 70 times travel distance to sun from earth and back. That is the length of this structure, each chromosome in our body, which carries the law of our life, the genetic code that provides for us our life and maintains it. Every millimeter of it contains the vital information, the genetic code, stretched out into infinity. There is no other structure that the human race ever produced that can store this vast amount of information. Maybe future scientists might be able to do.

It is important to read the verse in Quran 18:109, "If all the sea were ink for my Sustainer's (God's) words, the sea would indeed be exhausted ere my Sustainer's (God's) words are exhausted! And (thus it would be) if we were to add to it sea upon sea."

It is not clear where God will decree to write this many words. There is nowhere on earth or places that human beings can explore any written document to represent God's statement about this writing in ink using sea as the ink pot. But it may be an allegorical, descriptive term for the vast vocabulary of God.

There are eighty-seven million different species, according to scientists. Each different species has a different genetic code to produce different proteins and enzymes. Could this genetic code written in alphabets represent the words of God mentioned in Quran above that cannot be written down before the sea of ink dries out? Or is it a reference to something else?

As we have advanced in science and in our exploration of space and the mortal human body, we have come across a vast system of biological information and storage system, written in four-letter sequences: A (Adenine), G (Guanine), C (Cytosine), T (Thymine), and that is the amazing human genome! When scientists looked at the human genome, a vast expanse of recorded information was found embedded in the complex matrix of chromosomes, proteins, and histones. If someone tries to write it down in ink and (probably paper as we understand how writing is done, my insertion) as mentioned in the above verse all the seas if converted into ink, may not be enough to finish writing all the genetic information contained in the human genome.

As described above, if the chromosomes and DNA matrix is uncoiled and tied end to end, it will traverse the distance from earth to sun and back seventy times and that distance is 93,000,000 miles multiplied by 70, which is beyond human comprehension. On these chromosome fibrils are DNA that contains the genetic code, junk DNA (non-coding DNA) and DNA from previous species. And if anyone can write all these down-all the base pairs and the genetic code from all the chromosome fibrils in our body on paper with ink one might need all the seas turned into ink to complete it as mentioned in Quran 31:27 and 18:109. That much information is stored in our body, in the cells in our genome.

These verses in Quran is a strong reference to the human genome and the genetic code.

THE DOUBLE HELIX-DNA

In 2003, the initial human genome sequencing was published. Scientists have not completed the sequencing of the entire genome. There may be novel information as to our past and probably the future of human beings, which will be evident when the genome is fully studied.

The DNA and the genes, under the influence of epigenetics, control our life, our actions, thoughts and behaviors, and become the basis and ultimate cause for our fate or predetermination or Al-Qadar in Arabic.

As Yusuf Ali comments on this verse, God's words and mercy are in all creations. Quran:18:109.

In this context, we will look at another verse in Quran, which refers to the heavenly tablet " ". Al-Lawh means anything written on, flat surface, shoulder bone of an animal on which something is written and flat wood. Quran also says it is well protected. Both the Bible and Quran refer to the heavenly books where God's decrees are recorded.

This could be a reference to the human chromosome, the double helix, which is flat but twisted to look like a twisted ladder. (See picture.) There is information about our future, death, our actions and thoughts, and our fate in our genome. It is well protected. It is in the nucleus of the cell, protected by the nuclear membrane, cytoplasm, endoplasmic reticulum, and other organelles. It is wrapped in histones. Overall, it is covered by the skin. Additionally, the information inscribed in it is protected from cellular damage by cell division, by which the parent cell divides into two daughter cells and replicating the DNA so that the full complement of the DNA that was present in the parent cell is transferred into the daughter cells, whenever the parent cell is damaged.

DNA Double Helix

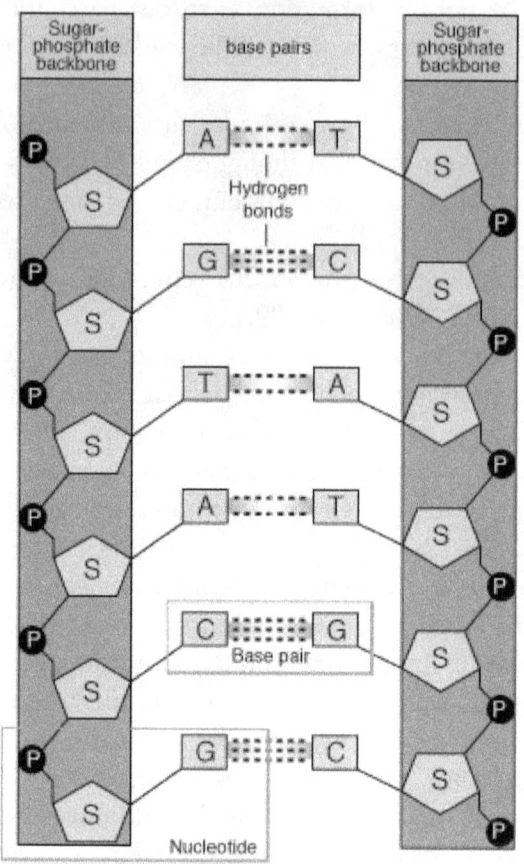

Credit: Office of Science Education and Outreach of the National Human Genome Research Institute

This figure is a diagram of a short stretch of a DNA molecule which is unwound and flattened for clarity. The boxed area at the lower left encloses one nucleotide. Each nucleotide is itself make of three subunits:

- A five carbon sugar called deoxyribose (Labeled S)

- A phosphate group (a phosphorous atom surrounded by four oxygen atoms.) (Labeled P)

- And one of four nitrogen-containing molecules called nucleotides. (Labeled A, T, C, or G)

Fig. 14

THE DOUBLE HELIX-DNA

In addition, the DNA and genes are protected by a process of "proofreading," during cell division Rarely a mistake can occur during cell division that affects the DNA. The error rate is roughly one in a billion so that the information in the chromosome is well protected as mentioned in Quran.

CHAPTER 12

Gene Transfer

Before we discuss the effects of mutations on the offspring, let us briefly discuss how the genetic information is transmitted to the offspring. The information in the gene or genome is written out in a linear and sequential chain of chemical building blocks called the nucleotides, also called the genetic letters, like the words in a printed document. These building blocks abbreviated as A, C, G, and T being the first letter of the name of the base, is carried in the chromosome, which is present in the nucleus of the cell. These building blocks form a continuous chain called deoxyribonucleic acid (DNA). These genetic letters are not connected side by side but are connected to a long backbone structure that runs the length of the DNA. This can be likened to the cross ties of a railroad where the ties are tied to the rail. DNA is referred to as a double helix. It consists of a pair of DNA strands with two backbones parallel to each other like railroad tracks and the bases pointing toward each other inward to contact the bases on the opposite strand and to connect with the backbones like the ties that are connected to the parallel railroad tracks (picture).

The genetic information is stored in the sequence of bases along the nucleic acid chain. The double helix in the living cells is not flat but looks like a twisted ladder see (picture). During cell division, the chromosome splits into two halves and these halves get similar complementary halves. When the cell divides and becomes two different

THE DOUBLE HELIX-DNA

cells, each cell will have the same genetic information as was in the parent cell and will have forty-six chromosomes.

This process of cell division is needed to repair and replace damaged cells or to repair tissues that are damaged. The base pairing results in the double helix. The base pairing provides a mechanism for copying the genetic information in an existing nucleic acid chain to form a new chain. The DNA is replicated by the action of an enzyme called DNA polymerase. This specific enzyme can create a copy of the DNA strand from nucleic acid templates with an error rate of less than 1 in 100 million nucleotides. This is an extremely fail-proof system.

Genes specify what kind of protein or enzymes is to be made, but DNA itself is not the direct template for protein synthesis. The template for protein synthesis is the RNA (ribonucleic acid) molecules. A class of RNA called the messenger RNA (mRNA) is the information-carrying intermediates in protein synthesis.

DNA Replication

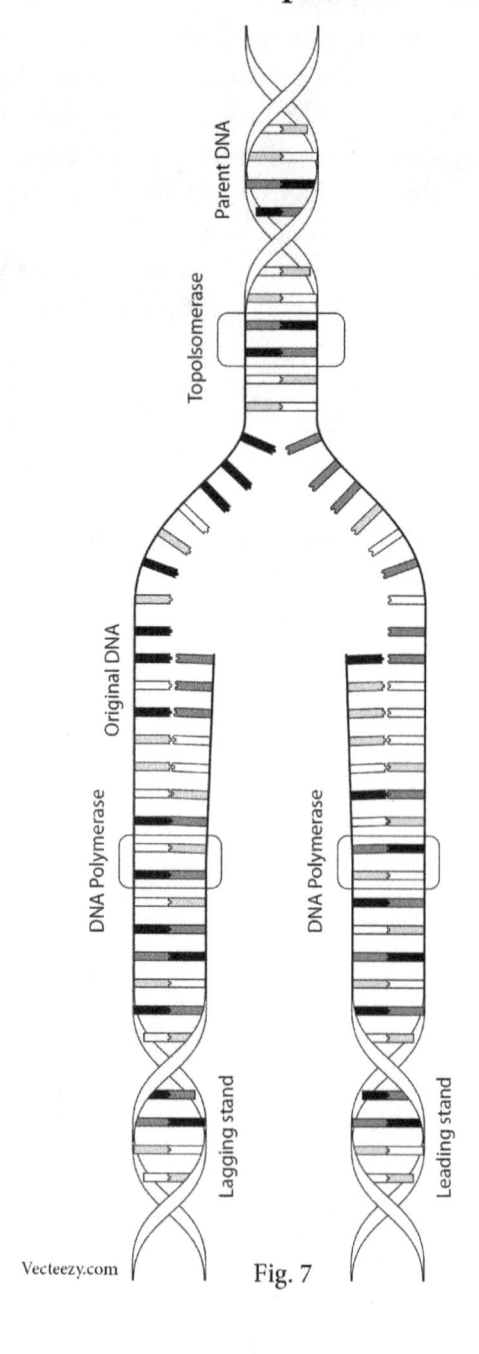

Fig. 7

Birth Defects

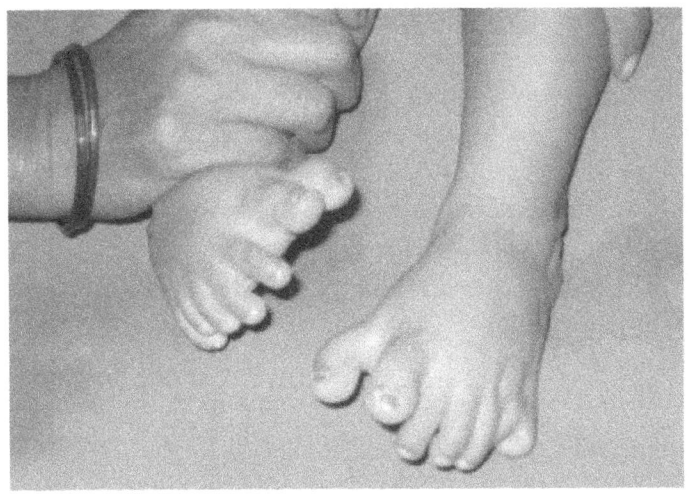

Credit: Gopalakrishna A, Jinka R, Kumar T S, Khan BA, Mevada K. Joubert syndrome with cleft palate. J Cleft Lip Palate Craniofac Anomal [serial online] 2014 [cited 2018 Mar 3];1:59-61. Available from: http://www.jclpca.org/text.asp?2014/1/1/59/126573

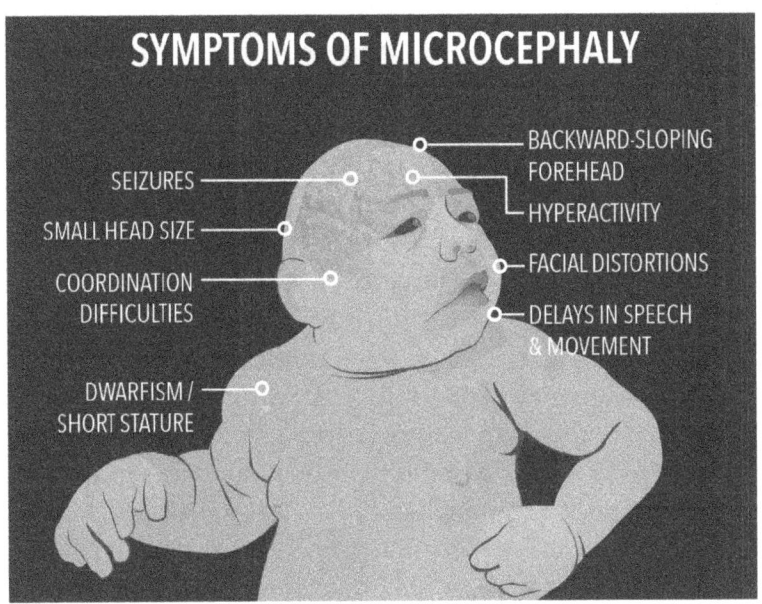

Credit: Beth.herlin (Own work) [CC BY-SA 4.0 (https://creativecommons.org/licenses/by-sa/4.0)], via Wikimedia Commons

Fig. 12

There are other RNA molecules like transfer RNA (tRNA) and ribosomal RNA (rRNA), which are part of the protein synthesis machinery. The RNA polymerase takes instruction from DNA templates. This process is called the transcription, and this is followed by translation that culminates in protein synthesis according to instructions given by mRNA templates. The genetic code is nearly the same in all organisms: a sequence of three bases called a codone, specifies an amino acid. Codones in mRNA are read sequentially by tRNA molecules, which serve as adaptors in protein synthesis. The synthesis of proteins takes place in ribosomes, which are made of complex rRNA and more than fifty kinds of proteins.

What about the genetic information transfer to the offspring? This is accomplished through the sperm and ovum called the germ cells. Each germ cell carries half of the chromosomes, twenty-three instead of forty-six, and when sperm and ovum meet in fertilization, the ensuing cell—the gamete—gets the full complement of chromosomes; that is, forty-six of them. In this process, the offspring gets DNA from both the parents and that is why the offspring looks different from each parent as the offspring gets a mixture of the genetic information from the father and mother. This process of fertilization carries the genetic information from the parents, including the mutant variety to the child, and the mutant gene can express in the child whether it is harmful or helpful.

If it is harmful, it can affect the internal biochemical function of the body or the external appearance of the child as a deformity, skin color change, or height, etc. This is what we call congenital defects when it is manifested in the physical appearance in childhood. This phenomenon of gene expression resulting in disfigurement of the child or adverse metabolic consequences due to harmful mutations is referred to as fate or predestination by God or Qadar in Arabic, and it is widely accepted by all religious factions, more so in the Muslim community.

But as you have seen, all these aberrations inside and outside our body, physical or biological, are a result of the changes in the genetic code due to changes in the sequence of the nucleotide called mutations. These are not an individual punitive decision or

THE DOUBLE HELIX-DNA

decree by the Creator as a punishment. In the Abrahamic faith and Zoroastrianism, the final judgment and punishment happens after death and resurrection and God will not accord punishment at random before the arrival of the final judgment day and much less on an innocent child who has not started his life yet.

In Hinduism, it is possible to have punishment on earth based on karma, in that if someone is cruel and antisocial, he or she can be punished with different modes, including lower life-forms in rebirths including birth defects. Here epigenetics may have a place. Epigenetics is the outside influence on genetic expression, in that if someone has a harmful mutation and if he or she practices a good lifestyle and is an ideal member of society and civilized, it might mitigate or reverse the harmful expression of the concerned gene.

Therefore, there is no reason to believe that these birth defects are random decisions of God for whatever reasons He may find it fits, but all these abnormalities, including our behavior, can be explained on the basis of genes and genetic abnormality. In other words, our form, color, behavior, and the internal milieu, organ function or dysfunction are originated and maintained by the directions given by the chromosomes, genes, and proteins the genes code for, even though we are taught that nothing happens on earth without the knowledge and permission of God. Even the falling of a leaf is believed to be with the permission of God (Quran 6:59). This also can be explained on the basis of the DNA as all living things have a predetermined genetic makeup as prescribed by God and at the appropriate time a leaf can fall when its function is accomplished, or a fly can die when its lifetime has passed. This does not mean that God will keep record of these happenings nor He orders the falling of a leaf or the death of a fly each time it happens. These are phenomena consistent with the law of nature established by God. Not that He cannot keep a record of these seemingly insignificant happenings, of course, as He is all powerful and all knowing.

In order to understand the basic tenets of predestination from a scientific angle, we need to look at the basic unit of life in our body that is the human cell where all the secrets of this phenomenon of predetermination are hidden. As described in Quran 6:59, "With

Him are the keys of the unseen, the treasure, that none knoweth but He. He knoweth whatever there is on the earth, in the sea. Not a leaf doth fall but with His knowledge. There is not a grain in the darkness (or depths) of the earth nor anything fresh or dry (living or dead) but is inscribed in a record clear (to those who can read)." This might be interpreted as the information contained in the law of nature that scientists can explore to see the depths of the earth and the sea or the information contained in the chromosomes, the generic code as we are exploring now.

There is mention of the dead or living in the verse above, which could represent the information about our life and death, which is encoded in the DNA in our genome. This information was unknown to man until the human genome was published and examined in 2001. The above verse also refers to "those who can read," which is referring to those who are knowledgeable about genetics. In this respect, our actions, behaviors, life, and death are already prerecorded in the DNA.

Those phenomena that afflict us physically, mentally, or any other manner all can be explained on the basis of our genes except those due to accidents, natural disasters, or wars. Even certain infections or the lack of it may have some genetic implications, which we can easily blame on fate or predestination or Al Qadar in Arabic.

Let us briefly review the beginning of our life in the mother's womb. Life begins with fertilization in which an ovum from the female gets fertilized by the sperm, and the resultant cell is called a zygote. The ovum has twenty-three chromosomes with XX female chromosomes and the sperm has twenty-three chromosomes with XY chromosome. Human cells have forty-six chromosomes. When the sperm and ovum get fertilized, the resulting zygote will have forty-six chromosomes. Only one sperm can enter the ovum and immediately after the first sperm gets inside the ovum, due to some chemical reactions, the wall of the ovum gets sealed so that no other sperm can get inside the ovum. After fertilization, the zygote rapidly divides, and when it reaches one hundred cells, it is called a blastula. The blastula becomes a blastocyst with a mss of cells in the center and an outer layer called the trophoblast. The inner cell mass becomes the embryo. The inner cell mass contain the embryonic stem cells that differentiate into different organs. The trophoblast becomes the placenta. The cells in the blastula rearranges into three layers. The outer layer becomes the ectoderm. The ectoderm gives rise to the nervous system and the epidermis of skin. The middle layer becomes the mesoderm that will give rise to muscles and connective tissue. The lower layer of cells become the endoderm that gives rise to the internal organs. These chromosomes reside in each cell in the nucleus. The chromosomes contain genes that are responsible for transmitting the traits, physical appearance, composition of internal organs, life span and our social behavior, and every aspect of life in the offspring.

When a woman gets pregnant, the first thing that the parents want to know is its sex, male or female. Years ago, it was impossible to say if the child was male or female, but now with ultrasound, one can determine the sex when the fetus shows markings of external genital organs. But up until week six of gestation, it is called the sexually indifferent period as the fetus can become a female or male depending on what hormones are secreted, especially the testosterone. If the fetus has Y chromosome and SRY gene, it will secrete testosterone and the child is destined to be male. On the other hand, if the XX chromosome is present, it will secrete estrogen and then the child becomes a female.

After fertilization for six weeks, the embryo is in a no man's land in terms of sexual differentiation. This period is called the indifferent or bipotential stage of gonadal development. The urogenital ridge is the precursor of the urinary and genital system. Each urogenital ridge divides into a urinary and an adreno-genital ridge in the fifth week. The gonadal ridge is bipotential and can develop into an ovary or testes. Gonads are subsequently colonized by primordial germ cells of extra gonadal origin.

In the Y chromosome, there is a gene called SRY (sex-determining region on the Y) and is established as the testes determining factor. But later on the transcription factor, SOX9 is considered the most important in determining testes. The existence of the testes determines the sex of the fetus and is called the sex-determining factor and the presence of ovaries does not influence sex differentiation. When no testes is present, the fetus becomes female.

Here, let me briefly introduce a paragraph from Quran, which has been put into controversy. The Quran 31:34 says, "Verily with God alone alone rests the knowledge of when the Last hour will come, and He it is who sends down rain and He alone who knows what is in the womb."

One controversy is based on the mistaken understanding and misrepresentation of the above statement. The critics took the statement that God alone knows what is in the womb to mean that God alone knows the sex of the fetus, which can be determined by physicians by the use of an ultrasound examination after seventeen to twenty weeks of gestation and not limited to God. But this Quranic statement never mentioned that God alone knows the sex of the fetus in the womb.

This verse in Quran refers to the unknown potential of the fetus when it becomes a full human being. That involves his color, height, intelligence, mental aptitude, a wise person or a criminal, an intelligent or less intelligent, a saint or a crook—in other words, the qualities of a human being. These characteristics of the would be human being cannot be determined in utero, by any scientific tests that are available now, and the influence of epigenetics on the future human being is unknown.

Even in sex differentiation as discussed earlier, up to six to seven weeks, the sex is in the indifferent state and we cannot determine the sex by available tests during that time. This can be the intent and meaning of the above referenced verse in Quran.

Quran 23:12–14 also gives a clear description of embryonic development exactly as described by science. In a Hadith (the sayings of the Prophet), it is mentioned that an angel descends on the fetus around forty-two days of gestation and writes down everything about the future of the individual. It consists of his longevity, death, livelihood, whether he or she be a good person or bad. In addition, the sex also is decreed. This statement reflects the total organogenesis of the fetus at age forty-two days of gestation, as described by the science of embryology. It is at this period in gestation that sex differentiation occurs according to science. As mentioned earlier, till week six of fertilization, there is a period of sex indifference. At week seven, due to testosterone secreted by the developing testes, the fetus becomes a male. This time corresponds to what is declared by the Prophet's statement about sex differentiation. The description of the angel's inscription of the future events of the growing fetus including the sex is nothing but the influence of the DNA, the hormones, and the chromosomal structure of the human cell.

In some descriptions of angelic forces, it is mentioned that they may represent the invisible forces that control the law of nature. If we apply that meaning of angelic forces, namely "the invisible forces," then we may relate the invisible forces like the electrical activity, enzymatic activity, and other metabolic activities in our body to angelic forces. Therefore, the angelic forces that record the sex of the fetus at day 42 of gestation may be the invisible force of testosterone that determines the sex of the fetus as described above.

Quran 31:34 says, "Only God knows what is in the womb." It does not specifically say the sex of the infant. It probably refers to the nature of the would-be person when he or she grows up, in terms of his behavior, his or hers disposition, social or antisocial temperament, his financial status, or his or her accomplishments, before the infant is born and becomes an adult. If it is related to the knowledge of the sex of the fetus, till six to seven weeks of gestation, sex determination is impossible based on the scientific knowledge we possess but God is capable.

Many of the abnormalities are obvious at birth or soon after, and we call them due to fate or predetermination with the inner meaning of a punishment from God. In Arabic, it will be called Al-Qadar. We believe in a Creator who is kind to human beings and one cannot agree with the notion that God created these abnormalities as a punishment, especially for an innocent infant. We also believe that punishment comes after final judgment after death. Moreover, many of these defects can be treated including gene therapy. If it was a decree from God, how can human beings correct it?

The causes of these abnormalities are due to mutations in the genes, and that process has been going on since the first appearance of the unicellular organism about 3.5 billion years ago, as described earlier. Some mutations are harmful and can lead to death of the offspring. Other mutations are beneficial, and it is due to the beneficial mutations that human beings are strolling the earth today, so long after starting out as the unicellular organism. There are over six billion human beings on earth, and each human being is different from the other, even among children of the same parents. This has avoided the monotony of seeing the same faces all over the world and is due to changes in gene expression or alteration in gene composition during fertilization.

Thus, all the abnormal looking births and the so-called "normal" human beings are fashioned out of the genetic code that resides in our body. Yet the belief that these are due to fate or Al-Qadar can give people some mental stress relief as it is considered as a divine decree and is beyond the capacity of the mortal human being to thwart it.

See some pictures of birth defects.

CHAPTER 13

Genetic Control of Our Thoughts and Actions

Does God interfere in our day to day life, our actions and behaviors, or is it the DNA and genes that dictate our activities, realizing that God is the originator of all causes? We know that everything we do, our behavior, and thoughts are based on DNA and the genes. The believers ascribe all these, namely the DNA and genes are by the work of God and consequently everything is directed by God. But we can say that God is not telling us what and when to do certain things or direct our success or failure or even death. These are based on our genetic makeup and expression. When we look at identical twins separated at birth and look at their behavior, it is known that they do exactly the same things on a daily basis even though they live miles apart.

James Springer and James Lewis are the famous twins who were separated at one month of age, adopted by different families and were reunited at age thirty-nine. When University of Minnesota psychologist Thomas Bouchard met them in 1979, he noted they shared interest in mechanical drawing and carpentry, their favorite school subject had been mathematics, and their least favorite subject being spelling. They smoked and drank the same amount and got headaches at the same time of day, suggesting the driving force is their DNA.

In schizophrenia, 50 percent will share the disease in identical twins but only 10–15 percent in fraternal twins. This difference is a strong indication of a genetic component for susceptibility in schizophrenia. This illustrates the genetic influence in diseases that affect us.

Other studies at the Minnesota Center for Twin and Family Research report that many of our traits are more than 50 percent inherited, including obedience to authority, vulnerability to stress, and risk taking. Even for issues like religion and politics, our choices are more determined by our genes than we think.

But even though genes are the basis of our body function and behavior, the determining factor in the final execution of any actions or behaviors is not only based on genetic makeup but also greatly influenced by the epigenetic factors or nurturing influences. A lot of what we are is a product of the DNA and the influence of nurture as well.

We see from archeology and history the gradual evolution of society apart from the biological evolution of species. After the separation of humanoids 1.5 million years ago, we see the Neanderthals who died off, probably due to the appearance of the superior species called the Cro-Magnons. The Cro-Magnons appeared about twenty-five to thirty thousand years ago, then the Adamic people came into existence. With the introduction of cultivation and domestication of animals and settled life, the Cro-Magnons were replaced by the Adamic race. These successive generations had better skills than the previous ones, and were based on advantageous genetic mutations in the new arrivals, which conferred on them a better survival advantage.

Human beings have also changed in their social characteristics and governance over the centuries. To begin with, we had the clans, tribes, kings, countries, and nations. They were all concerned with the population of their limited territories. There were wars between these entities. But now we think globally. Similarly, 3.5 billion years ago the unicellular organism appeared on earth, and by the process of evolution, we the human beings appeared. This ingenious mechanism of chromosomes, DNA, and genetic information storage and

THE DOUBLE HELIX-DNA

transmission has stood the test of time. Had the mutation process not been incorporated into the original cell's DNA, this phenomenon of different speciation would not have happened including our human species' appearance on earth.

We, the believers, ascribe to the wisdom of Almighty God for the Big Bang and subsequent evolution of the universe and the evolution of biological species. Others will argue this process was due to some random occurrence, in that millions of unicellular organisms would have perished while trying to divide and reproduce; and because they did not end up with the right DNA base sequences or the right mechanism for replication of chromosomes and cell division and consequently no daughter cells could be produced, they were extinguished. The one who accidentally embarked on the right base sequences and replication process that successfully created daughter cells and propagated, this cell line survived and eventually became multicellular organisms and species and eventually human beings, an accidental conglomeration of events.

The DNA can mutate into beneficial or harmful genes. It also can change in its expression without changing the base sequence. Mutation can be affected due to chemicals in the cell, absorbed from outside, or damage to the cellular contents from radiation or oxygen radicals.

The epigenetics influence our behavior as well as our traits, as we have seen in the changes in our society over the centuries. On an individual level, we see the transformation of brutal human beings being changed to acceptable personalities.

Looking at religious books, one can see the conversion of tyrants to normal people. In Hinduism, we see Jambavan and Satrajit accept Lord Krishna's message. In Christianity, we see those people who originally despised Jesus eventually accept Him. In Islam, many earlier enemies of the Prophet accepted him and Islam. A notable one was Hamza, a mortal enemy of the Prophet becoming an ardent defender of Islam. Looking at recent events, the life story of Malcolm X in the U.S was a glaring example of the influence of epigenetics. He was imprisoned at the age of 19 due to involvement in drugs, alcohol and other criminal activities. In the jail he was introduced to the Nation of Islam and was influenced by it. In 1964, after going for Islamic pilgrimage Hajj and subsequent repentance, he became a changed man and became an inspiration to millions worldwide. He became an ambassador for peace and social uplifting of the downtrodden. This shows the beneficial influence of epigenetics.

Even though the genetic imprints did not change, their genetic expression changed due to social changes and changing of their own thoughts and freewill, and this change is brought about due to epigenetics. Therefore, gene expression can be changed by influences outside the base sequence.

CHAPTER 14

The Telomere
The Time Keeper of Death

In the human chromosome, the telomere is at the end of the chromosome pair to protect the damage to the chromosome and DNA during cell division. If the telomere gets damaged, the chromosome and DNA get damaged; the cell dies. When cells die, the organism also dies. Scientists believe that the health of telomere is an indication of a human being's health and longevity.

In the future, it is possible that scientists can predict a person's death or how long a person could live based on examination of the telomere. In a study published in the journal *Annals of Neurology* on November 2012, researchers from Harvard University have given a genetic basis for people who tend to sleep earlier and those who sleep later (night owl). Human beings have a biological clock that determines the sleep onset and wake-up times called the circadian rhythm. The researchers compared the wake-sleep behavior of their study population with their genotype (the genetic makeup). They discovered a single nucleotide near a gene called "Period 1" that varied between two groups that showed different sleep-wake behavior.

Human genes are made of four nitrogen bases—adenine, thymine, guanine, and thymine. At the gene site "Period 1," 60 percent of the people have the nucleotide base adenine (A) and 40 percent have guanine (G). This site affects the sleep-wake cycle of all human beings. People who have the A-A genotype wake up an hour earlier than those who have the G-G genotype, and those who have the A-G genotype wake up exactly in the middle. This discovery is hailed as a major step in the understanding of a single genotype in a large population to determine the time of day when people wake up or go to sleep.

The investigators then looked at the time of death in those who died among the study population and found that this same genotype predicted six hours of variation in the time of death. Those with the genotype A-A or A-G phenotype died just before 11:00 a.m., like most of the population, but those with the G-G genotype on the average just before 6:00 p.m.

There is a genetic connection to the time of the day when death occurs. (This is related to natural causes of death and not related to accidents or other calamities. Author's inference.) This finding of the time of death is limited to the time of the day and not the year or date of death. But eventually looking at the telomere decay some time in the future, scientists probably could predict the longevity of an individual.

As described above, cells die and consequently all living things die. We see this in plants like paddy, wheat, or corn and vegetables. When these living things reach their term, they shrivel and die; and at that time, any intervention like water and fertilizers cannot prevent their death. Similarly, human beings also perish. As we get older, our hair turns white, skin becomes wrinkled, memory declines, teeth fall out, eyes get dim, the function of internal organs declines, and finally dies. This is a consequence of senescence of the cell and autoptosis or programmed cell death. We cannot say that this death can be delayed by innovations in rejuvenating the telomeres and the DNA. Scientists are working on this. As we have seen, the shortening and damage to the telomere leads to chromosome damage and that leads to cell death and eventually the organism dies.

How long can a human being live? No one knows. The Bible (Genesis:5:5) says that Adam lived more than nine hundred years.

The maximum life expectancy of present day human beings is 130 years according to the Bible (Genesis 6:3). Quran does not mention the longevity of human beings. About death, Quran 16:70 says, "And God created you and causes you to die and of you there are some they are sent back to senility so that they know nothing after having known" (much). Also, Quran:30:54 says, "God is He who created you in a state of weakness, then gave you strength after weakness and after strength gave you weakness and grey hair." And Quran:3:185 says, "Every human being is bound to taste death."

These verses affirm the inevitability of death as determined by the chromosomes and DNA, and this can be called the fate (predetermination) or in Arabic Al Qadar. Al Qadar or fate or predetermination all can be explained on the basis of the information that we carry in each cell in our body. God does not interfere in our daily activities or future events unless it is dictated by the DNA. But of course, our activities can be changed based on our free will and if someone wants to follow the guidelines prescribed by society or the respective religions.

We need to examine from a scientific angle what we call "fate or predetermination or Al Qadar" in light of DNA and chromosomes.

CHAPTER 15

The Telomere (Continued)

The Angel of Death

We are programmed to die. Telomeres are structures found at the end of our chromosomes. These are sections of DNA found at the end of the chromosomes. In humans, the telomere sequence is TTAGGG. This sequence is repeated about three thousand times and reach up to fifteen thousand base pairs. Telomeres help to organize each of the forty-six chromosomes in our cell nucleus. They protect the ends of the chromosome like the plastic tip of shoelaces. In the absence of this cap, the chromosome may be sticking to other chromosomes or just like the shoelace get frayed (splits apart), without the plastic cap, the chromosomes also get frayed and will become dysfunctional.

The Chromosome
Telomere (The Angel of Death)

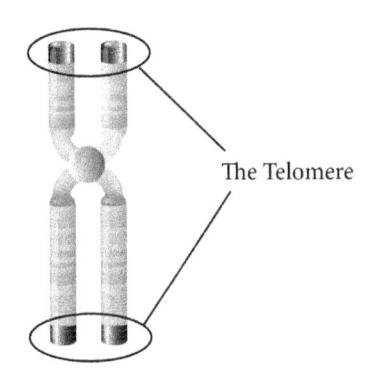

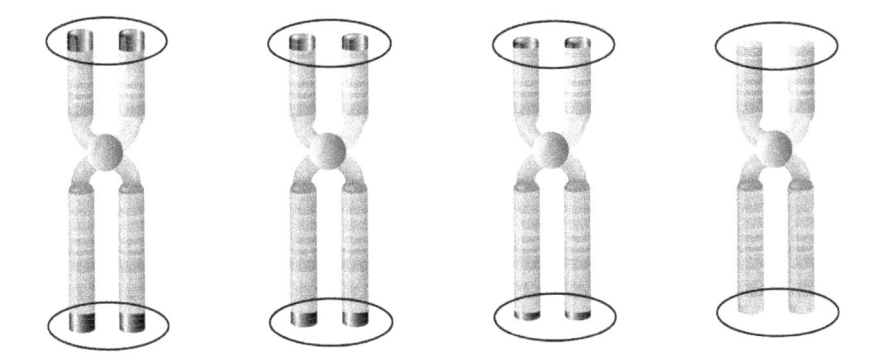

The Telomere

Due to repreated cell division and aging, the Telomere gets damaged and smaller and eventually the cell division stops and the cell dies.

Fig. 8

Telomeres allow replication of chromosomes in the proper fashion during cell division. Every time the chromosome replicates, the chromosomes are shortened by about twenty-five to two hundred bases—A, C, G, T—per replication.

But because the chromosome ends are protected by the telomere the bases in the telomere are not lost, the chromosome DNA will be saved. Without telomeres, important DNA will be lost every time a cell divides. Usually a cell divides about fifty to seventy times. This will lead to loss of most genes since each time a cell divides, twenty-five to two hundred bases are lost from the ends of the telomere on each chromosome, which leads to shortening of the telomeres.

Oxidative stress leads to loss of fifty to one hundred base pairs per cell division. Oxidative stress is caused by poor diet, smoking, obesity, lack of exercise, and stress. When the telomere gets too short, the chromosome reaches a critical length and can no longer be replicated and cell division stops. This critical length triggers the cellular death, called a programmed death or apoptosis. In life, the enzyme telomerase repairs and adds the TTTAGGG telomere sequence to the ends of chromosomes to prevent their shortening. But this enzyme is in very low concentration in somatic cells. This leads to aging of cells and deterioration of cell function, thereby the body also ages.

Mouse models lacking the enzyme telomerase were found to show signs of premature aging, as this enzyme prevents shortening of telomere. Therefore, telomere acts as the aging clock in every cell. Newborn babies have telomeres ranging in length from around eight thousand to thirteen thousand base pairs. Each year this declines by around twenty to forty base pairs. By the time someone reaches age forty, he or she would have lost up to 1,600 base pairs and the telomere gets shortened.

Short telomeres are connected to premature cellular aging. Telomere length represents our biological age as opposed to chronological age. Many scientific studies have shown a strong correlation between short telomeres and cellular aging. Similarly, the age related decrease in our immune function is also related to telomere shortening.

THE DOUBLE HELIX-DNA

There are several indications that telomere length is a good predictor of life span.

If there is abundant telomerase enzyme, aging can be postponed. There is abundance of telomerase enzyme in cancer cells, sperm and egg cells. That is why cancer cells multiply and grow uncontrollably. Therefore, the shortening of the telomere is a red flag to declare that the cells are deteriorating and ready to die and a declaration of approaching death of the individual. This deadly information is in the tiny cell in our body. To the believers it is the divine decree and to others it is just a physiological event. Quran 1:145, "And no human being can die save God's leave at a term pre-ordained" (Asad).

"No one can die before his appointed term except in accordance with the law of God" (Ahmed Ali).

Quran 57:22 "No calamity can ever befall the earth and neither your own selves, unless it be (laid down) in Our decree before We bring it into being."

Quran 3:185 "Every human being is bound to taste death."

Quran 6:2 "He it is Who created you out of clay, and then has decreed a term (for you) a term known only to him." (Asad)

"It is He who created you from clay, then determined a term (of life) for you" (Ahmed Ali).

This divine decree of death is inscribed in our body, in the chromosome in the form of the telomere and this process of genetic decree is ordained long before our birth, through the transfer of genetic information, through reproduction, generation after generation.

CHAPTER 16

Our Phenotype (Physical Appearance)

Human beings have spread out over five continents and there are over six billion of them, yet no one is exactly like the other one in appearance except identical twins. There are black-, white-, or brown-colored people. We generally consider this phenomenon is due to God's decision. We attribute everything to the will of the Almighty. But science-oriented people and researchers try to find an acceptable scientific basis for all phenomena in the universe including those that affect human beings, whether it is the skin color or other physical and mental aberrations notwithstanding the fact that all causations are ultimately decreed by God. The believers in general attribute anything that happens to human beings as the will of God and His predetermination and contend with it.

When children are born and live their lives, each will have a different appearance, mannerisms, color, height, level of intelligence, as well as behavior that are different from the others. But we do not give much attention to these minor deviations from the others unless they are very obvious like dwarfs—too tall, too black, or too white or blue or red eyes, or extra fingers, stammering, deaf-mutism, etc., and then we call it as the will of God or predestination or in Arabic Al Qadar. Still more obvious defects like anencephaly (undeveloped brain), Down's syndrome, deformed body parts or conjoined twins etc we see in our society. All can be explained on the basis of genetic mutations and expression in the DNA of the cells in the body.

Of course the human body was created by the supreme God, beginning at the Big Bang with dust and the ensuing biological evolution, but one cannot contend that these aberrations were ordered by God for those individuals when they were conceived. One can blame the Almighty as He is the cause of all causations. But in this book, my attempt is not to assign blame to one entity or the other but to explain these anomalies on the basis of genetic variations in the DNA and not to contend with the notion that these misfortunes are due to the result of random decision of God to express His displeasure with the affected individual. As God is merciful to all living things, it is hard to imagine such an entity deliberately engineering such horrendous maladies on human beings, especially on innocent children. We need to understand that God is not micromanaging the daily lives of human beings. This universe is built as a self-sustaining entity till the end of the world with the understanding that there will be raptures, calamities like earthquakes, floods, famine, epidemics, and the like according to the law of nature as prescribed by Him.

Some historic facts will support the realization that God will not intervene in the affairs and events that happen in the earth, not only for ordinary people, but also for people close to God, namely the prophets and their close associates. The Bible states that Jesus was tortured by His fellowmen to the extent that Jesus's face was disfigured and was crucified (Matthew 27:46) and Jesus cried out to God, "Why have you forsaken me?"

Islam does not believe in crucifixion or accept Jesus as a son of God and does not believe that Jesus died on the cross, but the Bible says that Jesus cried out to God (Father) to help Him, but nothing happened.

In Islamic history, Prophet Muhammad had a defeat in the battle of Uhud in third Hijra, against the forces of Abu Sufiyan. After the Prophet's death, the second caliph Umar Al-Khattab was assassinated by a Persian windmill maker who stabbed him with a knife, October 31 in AD 644, as the Caliph was leading morning prayer in the mosque.

The third Caliph, Uthman Ibn Affan, was murdered by a few Egyptians on July 20, 656.

The fourth Caliph, Ali ibn-Abuthalib, was murdered by an Egyptian named Ibn Muljam on January 26, 661, AD.

Hassan ibn Ali, grandson of the Prophet, died of poisoning by one of his wives in AD 670.

Hussayn ibn Ali, another grandson of the Prophet, was murdered in Karbala on tenth Muharram, being beheaded on October 10, 680, AD.

These were personalities who were championing the cause of Almighty (Islam) but were murdered, and there was no divine intervention.

We can also see either man-made calamities or natural disasters killing people at the sanctum sanctorum of worship in all religions. Whether it is a temple, church, synagogue, or a mosque including the events at the Grand Mosque of Mecca. In 2005, there was an earthquake measuring in the neighborhood of 7.6 on the Richter scale in northern Pakistan during the month of Ramadan, the holy month in Islam. But those God-fearing people in that region were not spared from death and destruction. These events are subject to the law of nature. Whether due to natural causes or otherwise, God will not intervene. Another example is the, death and destruction caused by the camp fire in California in the U.S.

Quran 13:11, "Thinking that he has hosts of helpers-both such as can be perceived by him and such are hidden from him-that could preserve him from whatever God may have willed. Verily, God does not change men's condition unless they change their inner selves, and when God wills people to suffer evil (in consequence of their own evil deeds) there is none who could avert it: for they have none who could protect them from Him."

We need to explore the inner meaning of this verse in two separate scenarios: (a) God does not change men's condition unless they change their inner selves? As you recall, human beings function physically and mentally through the action of DNA and genetics. We can change into a God fearing and sociable individual by good nurturing, avoidance of vicious thoughts and actions, prayers and repentance, which will have a beneficial impact on gene expression through epigenetics as shown by science. God won't order a change other than through the change in the DNA.

(b) When God wills people to suffer evil (in consequence of their own evil deeds) reiterates the fact through free will if people deliberately continue to do evil deeds, they have no chance to change, as the genetic expression cannot change as there is no beneficial epigenetic influence in them such as avoiding bad deeds and thoughts, to change to be sociable people, and such individuals are doomed for God's anger and punishment when they die. This primarily refers to change in our social and personal behavior and mental attitude and eventually the emancipation of the soul. This statement endorses the fact that people change only when the genetic expression changes ("the inner selves"—gene expression), due to good nurturing, good behavior, and godly acts. From this, we can conclude that God will not interfere in the day to day affairs or events that affect human beings, and it will be left to the law of nature established by Him, the DNA, and genes. Moreover, we can contend with the thought that anything that affects us individually like illness, infection, birth defects or death, everything other than due to natural disasters, epidemics, accidents, poisoning, or famine are all a direct effect of our DNA and the genes.

CHAPTER 17

Mutation

Gene mutation is a permanent alteration in the DNA base sequences. Mutation can be divided into two major classes:

Insertion Mutation

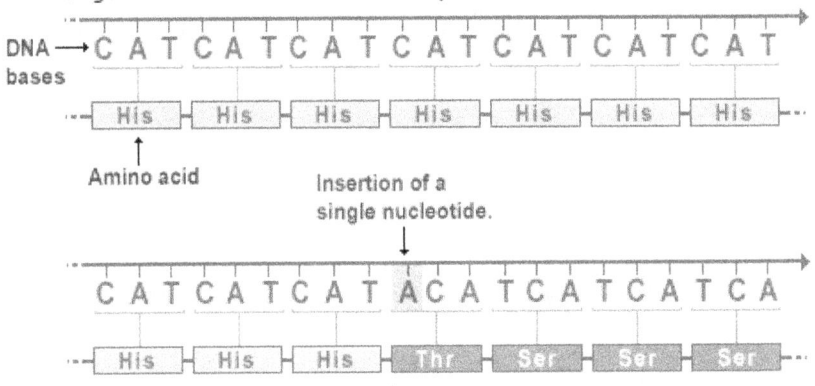

Original DNA code for an amino acid sequence.

DNA bases → C A T C A T C A T C A T C A T C A T C A T

His — His — His — His — His — His — His

↑
Amino acid

Insertion of a single nucleotide.
↓

C A T C A T C A T A C A T C A T C A T C A

His — His — His — Thr — Ser — Ser — Ser

Incorrect amino acid sequence, which may produce a malfunctioning protein.

U.S. National Library of Medicine

Nonsense Mutation

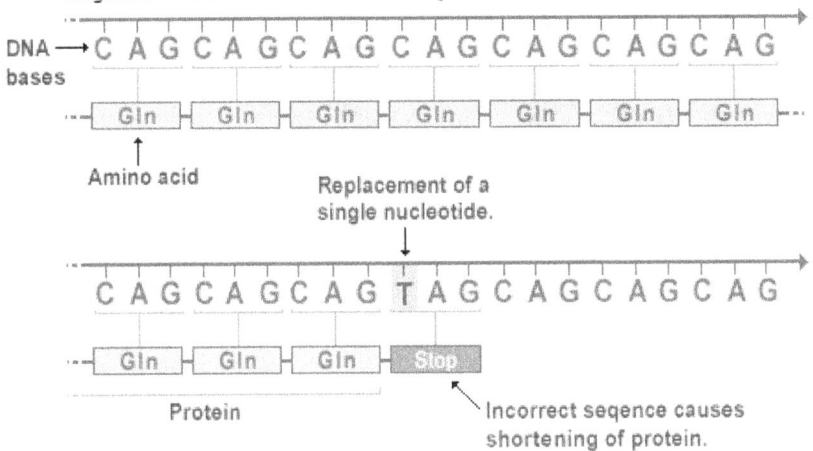

Original DNA code for an amino acid sequence.

DNA bases → C A G C A G C A G C A G C A G C A G C A G

Gln — Gln — Gln — Gln — Gln — Gln — Gln

↑
Amino acid

Replacement of a single nucleotide.
↓

C A G C A G C A G T A G C A G C A G C A G

Gln — Gln — Gln — Stop

Protein

Incorrect seqence causes shortening of protein.

U.S. National Library of Medicine

Fig. 9

Deletion Mutation

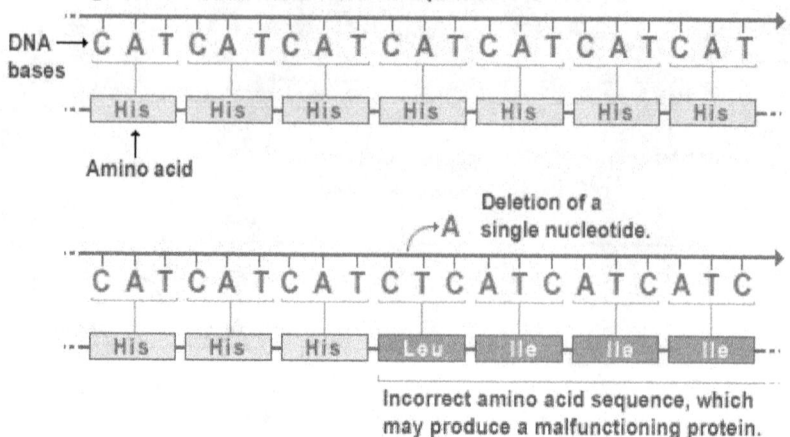

Original DNA code for an amino acid sequence.

DNA bases → C A T C A T C A T C A T C A T C A T

His — His — His — His — His — His — His

↑ Amino acid

Deletion of a single nucleotide. → A

C A T C A T C A T C T C A T C A T C A T C

His — His — His — Leu — Ile — Ile — Ile

Incorrect amino acid sequence, which may produce a malfunctioning protein.

U.S. National Library of Medicine

Repeat Expansion Mutation

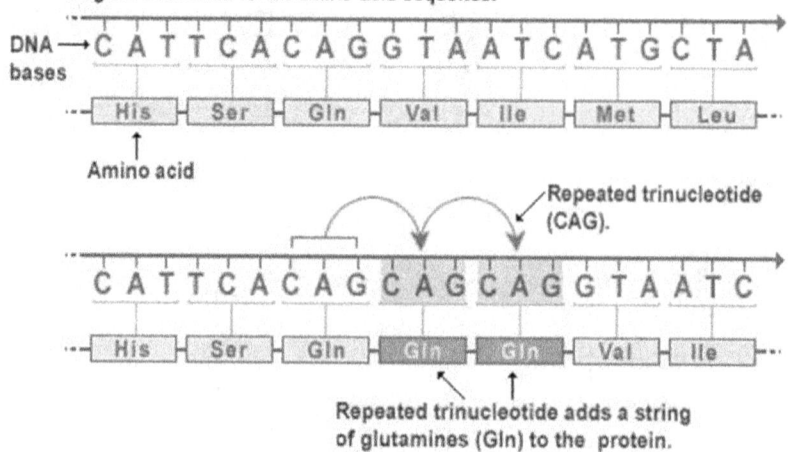

Original DNA code for an amino acid sequence.

DNA bases → C A T T C A C A G G T A A T C A T G C T A

His — Ser — Gln — Val — Ile — Met — Leu

↑ Amino acid

Repeated trinucleotide (CAG).

C A T T C A C A G C A G C A G G T A A T C

His — Ser — Gln — Gln — Gln — Val — Ile

Repeated trinucleotide adds a string of glutamines (Gln) to the protein.

U.S. National Library of Medicine

Fig. 10

Duplication

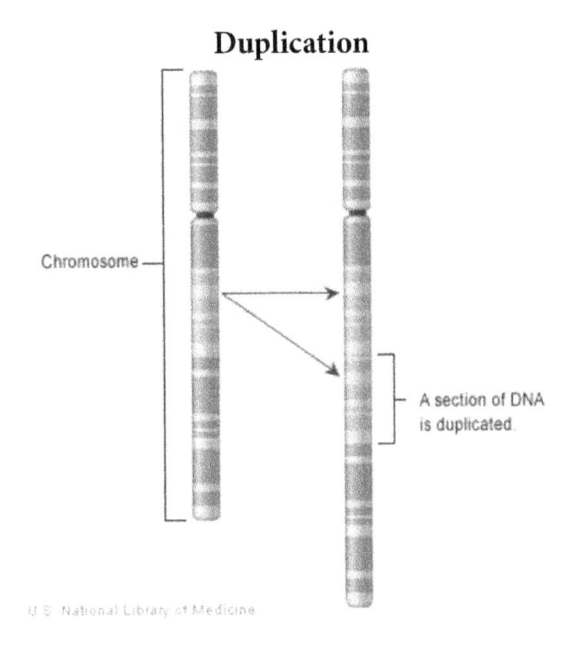

Chromosome

A section of DNA is duplicated.

Frameshift Mutation

Original DNA code for an amino acid sequence.

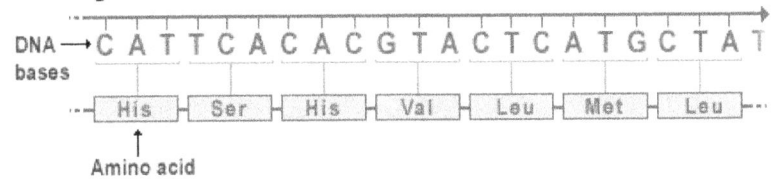

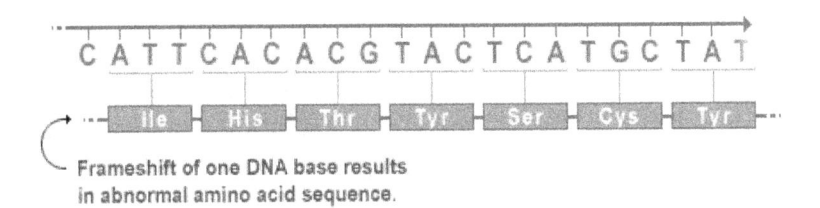

DNA bases → C A T T C A C A C G T A C T C A T G C T A T

His — Ser — His — Val — Leu — Met — Leu

↑ Amino acid

C A T T C A C A C G T A C T C A T G C T A T

Ile — His — Thr — Tyr — Ser — Cys — Tyr

Frameshift of one DNA base results in abnormal amino acid sequence.

Fig. 11

1. Hereditary: This mutation is inherited from the parent and is present in every cell of the person and persists throughout the person's life. These mutations are present in the sperm or ovum also called germ cells. This mutation will be carried by the offspring, generation after generations
2. Acquired mutation, or somatic mutation, occurs sometime in a person's life in certain cells and not in all the cells. This can be either as hereditary or somatic. These mutations are caused by environmental factors like radiation, ultraviolet light, chemicals, oxygen radicals, or base pairing errors. Mutation in somatic cells will not be passed to the next generation unlike mutation in germ cells like sperm or ovum.

Mutations are the rule in biological history. It is the beneficial mutations that ended up in the creature we call human being. Sometimes we see individuals with a gross abnormality like a cleft lips or something else, which is due to a harmful mutation. But we all have mutations in our genome that are not obvious and we consider ourselves normal, even though everyone looks different, other than identical twins.

What is normal in a human being? Who is normal and who is abnormal is all in the individual's mind except when someone is born with an obvious feature that is not seen in the majority of the population. We call it a defect and relegate it to predetermination or fate.

The human race evolved out of previous species due to beneficial mutations. We do not have a phenotypical description of the "first" human being or the "normal" human being. In the Judeo-Christian Islamic faith, the first human beings are believed to be Adam and Eve. In Hindu philosophy, it is believed to be Manu. But we do not have a physical description of them, so how does a "normal" ideal human being look like? Yet, despite the fact that every one of us is actually different from the other next to you, phylogenetically and genetically we do not look at the other as someone different. This fact does not come into consideration as we consider we are all "normal" unless a gross abnormality is evident.

THE DOUBLE HELIX-DNA

When we are faced with gross abnormalities as described in Chapter 19, the believers attribute that to his or her fate, predetermined by the Almighty or Al Qadar in Arabic, or in Hindu philosophy due to bad karma in previous generations.

We can make a scientific argument that these gross physical abnormalities are not the result of random punitive action of God, as He does not get involved in the daily minute by minute affairs on the earth and human beings and does not micromanage the events that we face every day. The events on earth can be explained by the law of nature and the events related to human beings can be explained by the control of our genes and DNA, whether it be a physical misfortune or a mental aberration.

As the universe works on certain preset laws established by the creator, as mentioned in Quran and Bible (Bible, Romans 2:14–15; Quran, 35:11), the events on earth work according to the law of nature. We quite often suffer from diseases or sustain accidents, and we are subject to the vagaries of nature, such as earthquakes, hurricanes, draughts, and famines or epidemics, and often we blame God for these maladies. The believers consider God as kind and merciful, however, and as such these maladies cannot be attributed to the Creator.

As far as death is concerned, which is the most dreaded event, it is prescribed for every living thing by God. No life form has evaded death. (Bible: Job; 14:5; Quran: 2:259; 6:60). It is established in our genes in the form of telomere when telomere deteriorates the chromosomes cannot replicate and the cells stop dividing and the cells die and the organism dies as well.

Telomere is at the end of the chromosome, like the plastic tip of a shoelace to prevent fraying of the end of the shoelace. Similarly, the telomere protects the end of the chromosome from fraying. When the telomere disintegrates due to repeated cell divisions, the chromosome cannot replicate and the cell dies. Looking at the damaged telomere, scientists can predict how long the individual can live. Telomere is the time keeper of death.

But how and when death occurs is not preordained. Some deaths will be due to accidents, some due to infections, some due to changes inside our body, chemical or biological.

Scientists and geneticists will be able to predict when death of a person will approach, by analyzing the telomere, in the cells, in the future.

CHAPTER 18

Genetic Diseases (Mutations)

Diseases related to genes—genetic diseases—are a result of the genetic variations in the DNA called mutations. The mutation can result from physical forces like radiation, chemicals that we consume, reactive oxygen radicals, stress, smoking, and other insults that our body is exposed to. This affects our physical body as deformities, cancer, or other birth defects or psychological aspects like aggression, schizophrenia, etc.

Our lifestyle has a lot to do with gene mutations. A case in point is the observation made by William Oschner, a physician, about lung cancer. He saw in a patient cancer of the lung. He immediately called all the medical students and other health professionals and said that this was a rare disease and they may not see another case like this in their lifetime, as it was a rare disease during the time of Dr. Oschner a hundred years ago. But now after a century, we see cancer of the lung on a daily basis. This is the result of mutation that has happened in genes from our lifestyle, namely smoking and exposure to radon.

Breast cancer is on the increase, and it is still defying a cure. Hereditary breast and ovarian cancer is associated with mutation in BRCA 1 or BRCA 2 gene. In the following chapter is a list of genetic disorders or illnesses due to gene mutations.

What is a mutation? Before we can understand the meaning of the word *mutation* we should know the genetic makeup of the living organism. The human cell contains a variety of formed and liquid materials of which the nucleus is the supreme structure that contains the chromosomes and the DNA, which is the maintainer and custodian of life and the functionality of the individual. In our body, cells divide to make new ones, to replace dead cells, or to repair damaged tissue. In this division the cellular contents, all of them should be divided and reconstituted to match exactly with the components of the parent cell. As you can see, the genes are in the chromosomes, and the chromosome is made like a twisted staircase. The DNA is made of four base pairs namely A, C, G, T, and each one is bonded with the other in a specific order. When cells divide and reconstitute, the chromosome is split in the middle by the enzyme polymerase, and it helps its reconstitution, in which the base pairing should be exactly as it was in the parent cell.

Remember there are three billion base pairs that have to be conjoined. In this process, some mistakes can happen in the order of one mistake in 10,000,000,000 replicated bases. But there is an inherent correction process to rectify the mistakes called editing and correction as we do in our printed media or books.

So, we have the genetic code in the DNA, which is carried in the chromosome helix. In order for the organism to be alive and functioning, the mere presence of the DNA in the chromosome is not enough. The phenomenon of life and the ability of the cells to maintain its function and consequently the life itself depends on the proteins and enzymes manufactured by the ribosomes in the cells. This is carried out by the genetic code in the gene that is in the DNA, which is the sequence of the bases in the gene. This code is transmitted into RNA called messenger RNA or mRNA. This information is then transferred to another RNA called transfer RNA or tRna. The tRNA transfers this information to the ribosomes in the cell, which manufactures the amino acid and which in turn produces the vital agent, the protein.

How is an abnormal (mutated) gene formed and transmitted to the offspring? What is a mutation? In human beings, a mutation means a change in the sequence of the base pairs of the DNA that determines the genetic blueprint. It represents a change in the sequence of bases that was present in the genes of the parents of that individual. In human beings, this change in the DNA could be in the the chromosome of the nucleus or in the mitochondria. The base pairs are made of four bases: A (Adenine), C (Cytosine), G (Guanine), and T (Tyrosine). These bases each pair up with a specific base on the other half of the reconstituting DNA helix and that format has been kept for over three billion years without change except when a mutation occurs. Mutation occurs when the sequence of base pair changes, for example A-T changes to C-G, or the deletion of a base pair occurs or insertion of a base or two.

There Are Different Kinds of Mutations:

Missense mutation. In this, there is a change in one base pair in the DNA, which results in the substitution of one amino acid for another in the protein made (code) by a gene.

Nonsense mutation: In this situation, even though there is a base pair substitution, the DNA sequence prematurely signals the cell to stop producing the protein, resulting in a shortened protein that may not function properly or not at all. This will affect the cell or the organism.

Deletion: In this kind, the number of bases are reduced in the DNA. Small deletions may remove one or a few base pairs within a gene while larger deletions can remove an entire gene or several adjacent genes. The deleted gene alters the function of the protein and can be harmful for the organism.

Duplication: In this, a piece of DNA is copied during cell division more than once and affects the function of the protein the DNA is coding for and will affect the well-being of the organism.

Frame shift mutation: A reading frame consists of groups of three bases that each code for one amino acid. The frame shift mutation shifts the grouping of these bases and changes the code for the amino acids. This results in a nonfunctional protein.

Repeat expansion: Nucleotide repeats are short DNA sequences that are repeated a number of times in a row. A trinucleotide repeat is made up of three base pair sequences and a tetra nucleotide repeat is made up of four base pair sequences and the resulting protein functions improperly.

Mutations can be due to errors of cell division and resultant chromosome duplication. The incidence of mutation due to error in base paring during cell division is approximately one in ten billion bases replicated. Most of them are inconsequential. This low rate of error is due to the extreme efficiency of the enzyme polymerase that helps chromosome duplication and insertion of base pairs.

The effect of any mutation is reflected in the nature of the amino acids and its sequence in the protein that will have on effect on your genotype and consequently your phenotype. It is the amino acids and the proteins that form the quintessential ingredients of our life and body.

Some mutations are harmful, others could be inert, and still others would be beneficial. It is the beneficial mutations that propelled the emergence of myriad different species based on the survival of the fittest when they acquire the beneficial mutations. Had there been no beneficial mutations, the world would be still ruled by the single cell organism without the species called humans.

CHAPTER 19

Birth Defects

A few birth defects that can be observed by our own eyes without genetic testing will be described. (These are due to genetic defects.)

Albinism	white skin (depigmentation) pink eyes, white hair	tyrosine def autosomal rec
Alkaptonuria	urine turns black on standing, dark nail	autosomal recessive
Angelman syndrome	mental retardation, ataxia, seizures	deletion short arm of ch 15
Ataxia-Telengectasia	cerebellar ataxia, telengectasia	autosomal

Cri du Chat syndrome	syndrome cry of the cat, mental retardation microcephaly, cat like cry, round face	5p deletion ch 5
cystic fibrosis	fibrosis symptoms: meconium ileus- blockage of bowel, chronic dough, failure to thrive, bronchiectasis, early death	CFTR gene defect, chrm 7
Digeorge syndrome	hypocalcemic tetany	3rd and 4th pharngeal pouch def
Down's syndrome	mental retardation, congenital heart disease	trisomy 21
Edward's syndrome	mental retardation, microphthalmia, cleft palate, lip, polydactyl, rocker bottom feet	trisomy 18
Ehler's-Danlos syndrome	laxity of joints, hyper extensibility of skin	Autosomal defect in collagen
Fabry's Disease	skin lesions, burning pain, cardiovascular and cerebral disease	x-linked

Fanconi anemia	short stature, microcephaly, hypogenitalism strabismus, thumb anomaly, mental retardation microcephaly	Autosomal recessive
fragile x syndrome	mental retardation, enlarged testes in male	male longer tan dem repeats,
Galctosemia	failure to thrive, cataracts, mental retardation, cirrhosis, death	galactose accumulation
Hartnup's disease	disease diarrhea, dementia, dermatitis, skin rash, ataxia	malabsorption of tryptophan
Hemophilia Von Willebrand disease	Hemorrhage, hematuria, hemarthrosis	x-linked Von Willebrand factor def
Hereditary hemorrhagic Telengectasia (Osler Weber syndrome)	Telangiectasia of skin and Mucus membranes	Autosomal dominant
Homocysteinuria	mental retardation, ectopia lentis, genu valgum	autosomal recessive

Huntington's Disease	Progressive Dementia, abnormal movements	defect in chr 4
Hurler's syndrome	gargoyle-like faces, mental retardation death by age 10	autosomal recessive
Jo's syndrome	high histamine levels, eosinophilia, staph abscess, eczema	gamma-interferon def
Lesch-Nyhan syndrome	hyperuricemia, mental retardation, Self-mutilation, spasticity	x-linked recessive
Maple syrup urine disease	mental retardation, death, person smells like maple syrup or burnt sugar	autosomal recessive
Marfan's syndrome	Arachinodactily, Aortic aneurysm ectopic lens	Fibrillin def
McArdle's disease	muscle cramps, weakness, myoglobinuria	muscle phosphorylase def

Neurofibromatosis	Multiple Neurofibromas (Café au Lait) spots pigmented hamartomas of Iris	NFI gene defect
Niemann-Pick disease	Death by age 3	autosomal recessive
Osteogenesis imperfecta	multiple fractures, blue sclera, deafness	defect in collagen.
Patau syndrome	mental retardation, microphthamia, cleft lip, palate, early death	trisomy 13
Phenyl ketonuria	mental retardation, blond hair, blue eyes mousy body odor (from phenyl acetic acid in urine and sweat)	autosomal recessive
Pompe's disease	cardiomegaly, early death	Glucosidase def
Prader-Willie syndrome	mental retardation, short stature, hypotonia, obesity, small hands and feet, hypogonadism	Short arm chr 15

Tay-Sachs disease	mental retardation, blindness, cherry red spot in macula, death by age 4	autosomal recessive
Tuberous Sclerosis	Tubers (glial nodules) mental retardation Adenoma sebaceum	Autosomal dominant
Turner's syndrome	amenorrhea, webbed neck, short stature coarctation of Aorta, infantile genitalia	non-disjunction of sex chr monosomy 45, x
Von Hippel-Lindau syndrome	hemangioblastoma of cerebellum, medulla or retina, cysts in visceral organs	Autosomal dominant
Xeroderma pigmentosa	Dry skin, melanomas, opthalmic and neurologic abnormalities	defect in DNA repair

Birth Defects

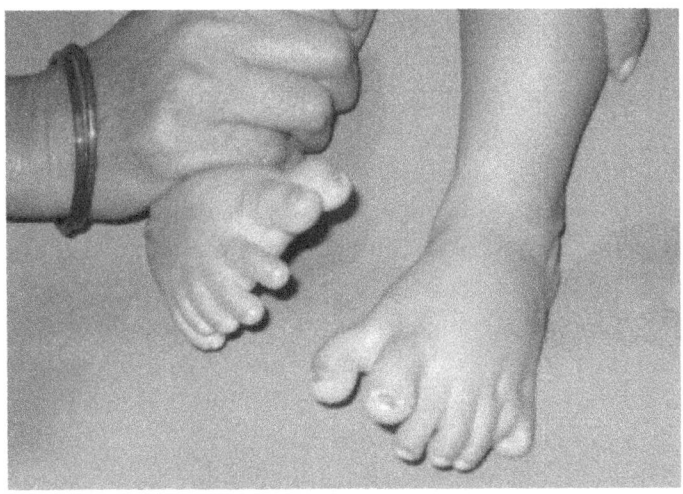

Credit: Gopalakrishna A, Jinka R, Kumar T S, Khan BA, Mevada K. Joubert syndrome with cleft palate. J Cleft Lip Palate Craniofac Anomal [serial online] 2014 [cited 2018 Mar 3];1:59-61. Available from: http://www.jclpca.org/text.asp?2014/1/1/59/126573

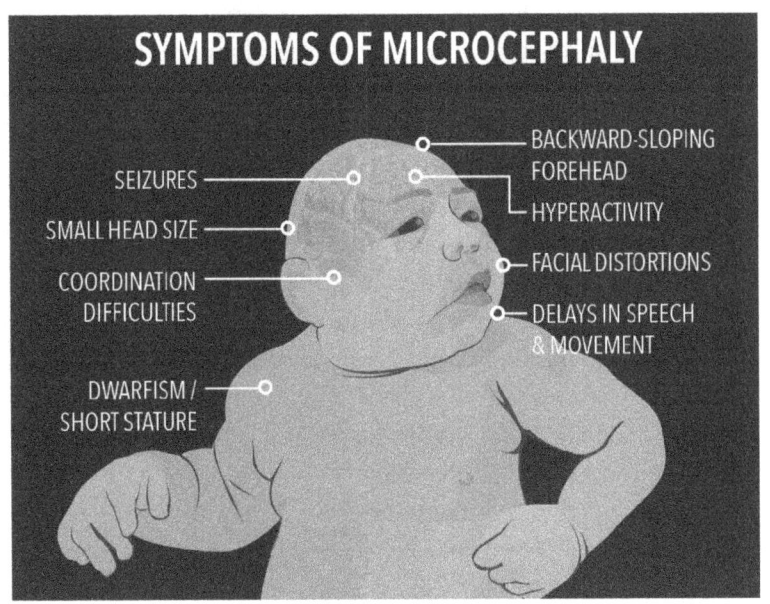

SYMPTOMS OF MICROCEPHALY
- SEIZURES
- SMALL HEAD SIZE
- COORDINATION DIFFICULTIES
- DWARFISM / SHORT STATURE
- BACKWARD-SLOPING FOREHEAD
- HYPERACTIVITY
- FACIAL DISTORTIONS
- DELAYS IN SPEECH & MOVEMENT

Credit: Beth.herlin (Own work) [CC BY-SA 4.0 (https://creativecommons.org/licenses/by-sa/4.0)], via Wikimedia Commons

Fig. 12

Many of these abnormalities are obvious at birth or soon after, and we consider these defects fate related or based on predetermination with the inner meaning of a punishment from God. In Arabic, it will be called Al-Qadar. We believe in a Creator who is kind to human beings and one cannot agree with the notion that God decreed these abnormalities as a punishment for the family for whatever they might have done against the wish of the Creator, through the hardship perpetrated on the infant. In Hindu faith, there is a belief that bad karma (activities) of an individual can result in a vicious form of rebirth as a punishment.

We (Abrahamic religion) believe that punishment comes after final judgment after death and not at birth. Moreover, many of these defects can be treated, including gene therapy. If it was a decree from God, how can human beings correct it?

The cause of these abnormalities are due to mutations in the gene and that process has been active starting from the unicellular organism 3.5 billion years ago. As described earlier, some mutations are harmful and can lead to death of the offspring. Other mutations are beneficial, and it is due to these beneficial mutations that human beings are strolling the earth today having started out as a unicellular organism about 3.5 billion years ago. There are over six billion human beings, each being different from the other, even among children of the same parents. This has avoided the monotony of seeing the same faces all over the world.

Thus, all the abnormal-looking births and the so-called "normal" human beings are fashioned out of the genetic code that resides in our body. Yet the belief that these are due to fate or Al Qadar in Arabic (random decree by God) can give people some mental stress relief as it is considered as divine decree and is beyond the capacity of the mortal human being to change it.

See some pictures of birth defects.

CHAPTER 20

What is death?

Regarding death as described earlier in chapter Mutation, it is ordained for all living creatures including human beings. Quran 22:5. for among you are such as are caused to die (in childhood) just as many a one of you is reduced in old age to a most abject state, ceasing to know anything of what has once knew so well. Just like life God has "created" death.

Quran 67:2. He has created death as well as life so that He might put you a test (and thus show) which of you is best in conduct, and (make you realize that) He alone is almighty, truly forgiving. Clinical death is defined as the cessation of all vital signs like heart beat, pulse, respiration and movements. But in 1960 the criteria for clinical death (as used by doctors and the legal system) was redefined with the addition of permanent and irreversible loss of consciousness due to cessation of brain stem activity (brain death). When brain death criteria is used to declare a person's death, it is not a biological death. Biological death means the cells in the body loses its metabolic activity and function and cannot be resuscitated. But in case of brain death the rest of the body can be salvaged and used for transplantation.

Quran 39:42. aptly describes sleep and death in a related fashion. God takes their soul at the time of their death and the soul of those who do not die, during sleep. He retains those souls for which He has ordained death whereas He releases the souls of the rest for an appointed time. Here the soul is described similar to life, consciousness or awareness. Those whose brainstem is dead and consciousness is irreversibly lost, their souls will not come back. During sleep awareness (consciousness) is lost temporarily and comes back when sleep is terminated. The permanent loss of consciousness (awareness) due to brainstem death is added in 1960 in the redefinition of death by medical professionals. In this scenario the mere absence of pulse, respiration and movements are not enough to call someone dead. The cessation of brainstem function should be ascertained and until such time he or she is not considered dead.

This principle is echoed in the verse in Quran 39:42. 1400 years ago, where it compares sleep to death, where the loss of awareness (consciousness) is temporary and in death it is irreversible due to death of brainstem. Scientists have now in effect established the human soul with human brain. (Princeton Journal of Bioethics. Medical Ethics. Nov 26, 2015). Other than accidents, poisoning, infections, and natural calamities, death is foretold by the degenerating telomere in the chromosome. In physiological terms death is permanent cessation of metabolic activity of the cells in our body. In the spiritual aspect it is the permanent separation of the soul from the body as described in Quran and the Bible.

According to a hadith (saying of the Prophet), the Prophet one day was sitting with his companions. He drew a line in the sand and said that their fate is already determined years before. Then the Prophet said when an infant is in the womb, four things are predetermined—one is death, second its provisions, whether he or she be a good person or bad. When the companions asked about free will, Prophet said those who want to strive for good He will facilitate it, but those who are bent on denying the truth He will let them do that and those who do good will have a beneficial outcome and those who indulge in bad things will have bad outcomes. This is exactly what science in the form of epigenetics describes, in that genetic expression can be altered by external influences. Epigenetics (external influences) won't change the genetic code, but its expression.

The above statement of the Prophet (Hadith) has tremendous scientific and genetic implication. The structure called the telomere

THE DOUBLE HELIX-DNA

at the end of the chromosome portends signs of death based on its damage and deterioration. It can be called the "angel of death" and as such we are programmed to die. The chromosome along with the telomere is passed on to generations after generations through sexual reproduction. We carry the copy of the chromosome and its end structure, the telomere from our forefathers who lived centuries ago, and the statement that our death is already decreed years before is very valid, as the telomere carries the genetic mechanism to foretell death and cause death as described earlier.

Here it is pertinent to read the verse in Quran 32:11, "The angel of death who is given charge of you, shall cause you to die, then to your Lord you shall be brought back." In this verse, it says the angel of death is given charge of you to suggest that we are under the control of this angel, which needs further clarification. In Judeo-Cristian-Islamic faiths the heavenly angel of death is known as Azrail and in Hinduism it is called Yaman or Kalan. Human beings are not under the control of angels, but of God. The angel of death is responsible to receive the RUH (life)/soul when we die and transport it for preservation till judgment day. The angel does not cause death either.

The angel's job is to take the soul when we die of any cause, and the angel does not cause our death. Therefore, the statement in the Quranic verse "the angel of death who is given charge of you" must relate to the telomere, which is the chromosomal segment that causes cell death and eventually the death of the organism (human beings). This scenario is for death due to natural causes. Death due to accidents, poisoning, and natural disasters are explained by other mechanisms, but the angel still takes hold of the life at the time of death.

This chromosomal part called telomere is in every cell of our body and can be considered to be in charge of us as it is responsible for maintaining the integrity of the chromosomes and controls the replication of the chromosome and being responsible for healthy cell division, which in turn helps maintain our body's functions for the continuation of our life.

When the telomere degenerates due to repeated cell divisions, the chromosome gets damaged and cell division stops and the cell dies and eventually the organism (our body) dies. Therefore, one can say that the telomere, the "genetic angel of death" is in charge of us as described in the above verse in Quran.

Angels only carry out the orders from God and are not agents of controlling human beings, as human beings are superior to angels as seen from verses in Quran. But one cannot compare angels and human beings and determine who is superior or inferior.

Angels are special creations of God to carry out certain tasks as ordered by Him. Nonetheless, certain verses in Quran will suggest that angels have no controlling authority over man.

Quran: 2:31, "And He imparted unto Adam the names of all things, then he brought them within the ken of the angels and said, 'Declare unto Me the names of these things, if what you say is true.'"

2:32, "They replied, 'Limitless art thou in Thy glory. No knowledge have we save that which Thou has imparted un to us. Verily, Thou alone art all-knowing, truly wise.'"

2:34, "And when We told the angels, "prostrate yourselves before Adam,' they all prostrated themselves save Iblis."

Quran 17:70, "We have honored the sons of Adam, provided them with transport over land and sea, given them for sustenance things good and pure and conferred on them special favors, above a great part of Our creations."

These chapters tell us that angels are not superior to human beings, and they cannot have a position to be in charge of our affairs including the heavenly angel of death—Azrail. Human beings are endowed with reasoning, judgment, and free will, which are not present in the angels. Additionally, in verse 2:30, God declares that Adam will be a Kalifa or vicegerent on earth who will represent God, confirming that human beings are superior to angels. The angel of death referred to in verse 32:11 must be the telomere of the chromosome and is a clear endorsement of God's creation of chromosomes and genes. Due to God-given qualities of human being, we are able to explore and discover the hidden biological marvels of chromosomes and genetics. This is a scientific endorsement of the saying that our death is predetermined through the involvement of telomere, which is the genetic foreteller of death (or the angel of death) and is carried by the offspring, generation after generation, through cell division and sexual reproduction.

The propensity to do good or bad is already dictated by our genetic code, but that alone is not enough to determine the final outcome. The epigenetics have significant influence on the genetic code expression and can alter the final outcome, and a genetic background for doing bad things can be altered into doing good things. There are ample examples of those stories involving enemies of society changing into very useful and productive individuals. There are ample examples of these in the religion of Hinduism and Judeo-Christian-Islamic faith.

This is the influence of epigenetics and is an undeniable endorsement of the sayings of the Prophet as shown above. All living organisms including human beings will die. Death is prescribed by the Creator according to the believers, and the scientists have discovered that natural death is due to decay of the telomere at the end of the chromosome, which causes the cells to cease dividing and leading to cell death.

Bible: Job 14:5, Quran: 7:34. Even in the absence of an accident, infection, poisoning or natural disaster, living organisms will die after an appointed time. Human beings die, crops die, and animals die and the death is determined by the degeneration of the structure at the end of the chromosome called telomere.

Our body structure both external and internal is fashioned by the genetic code. The abnormalities that we sometimes see at birth are due to mutations. We call such abnormalities fate, predetermination or Qadar in Arabic. The Arabic word *Qadar* means to create a plan, a design, and its execution. The end product of the plan is called Qala in Arabic, which in terms of DNA and genes is explained by the fact that the plan and instruction is in the genetic code (Qadar) and the end product of the plan and design is the protein and enzymes produced by the ribosomes in the cell. In the case of sexual reproduction, the Qadar (plan) is the meeting of the male and female gametes in the fallopian tube called fertilization, formation of the zygote, then the blastocyst, then the fetus and finally the baby, which can be called the Qala (end product) or the fate, and this entire process is predetermined and inscribed in the DNA and genes in the forty-six chromosomes.

As mentioned above, death also is prescribed for all humans. But how and where death will occur is only known to God. How and where is not predetermined as seen in the Quran. About the death of Prophet Muhammad, Quran 3:144 says, "And Muhammad is only a prophet, all the other prophets have passed away, before him: If, then, he dies or is slain will you turn about on your heels. But he that turns about can in no wise harm God, whereas God will require all who are grateful to Him."

Even in the case of the Prophet as described above, God did not predetermine how he might die, but death was prescribed. As shown in the above verse, the cause of death is left to the law of nature, either due to natural causes or due to violence like being killed in armed conflict, depending on the events that prevail in the locality, epidemic, natural disaster, starvation, war, etc. (according to the law of nature). as decreed by the Almighty. Quran 35:11, "it is God who created you from dust, then from a sperm, then formed you in pairs. Neither does a female conceive, nor gives birth without His knowledge, nor do the old grow older or become younger in years but in accordance with the Law of nature." (Ahmed-Ali).

At the time of the Prophet, there were several armed conflicts, imposed on the nascent Islamic community, and many believers including the companions of the Prophet were killed and in that context the Prophet also could have been "slain" as mentioned in the verse in Quran. The death is prescribed and predetermined as a function of the death of the telomere in the chromosome, but the cause of death is not predetermined. In other words, all deaths due to natural causes are due to damage and deterioration of the telomere and others are due to natural disasters, diseases, accidents, poisoning, etc. There is no reason to believe that God randomly decrees how a person should die, as discussed in the cause of Prophet's death.

As we see all around us, and as described in Quran, some die early and some very late in age; and this phenomenon has a genetic background without invoking God's random decision, at the same time recognizing the fact that the genetic aberrations are caused by the Almighty's design of genetic mutation. An individual can die at young age due to a harmful mutation in the gene or the mutation can reduce the resistance for infection or alter the metabolic function of the cell and cause death. And those who live longer will have beneficial alleles that make one live longer or can have resistance to infection or protect against heart disease or prevent dementia, etc.

It is believed that longevity is tied to genetic factors in 30 percent and the rest is due to the individual's lifestyle. The Seventh-Day Adventists in the US live five to eight years longer than the rest of Americans, and it is believed to be due to their lifestyle in that they exercise, eat a vegetarian diet, and abstain from smoking or drinking alcohol.

It is believed that over two hundred beneficial genetic alleles influence longevity. The important ones are the FOXO3A, IGFR-I, CETP variant, SRT1, TPS3, APOC3, AKT1, and IL6.

One Quran verse needs to be examined to understand the decrees of God regarding all the phenomena that happen in the universe and the disasters that happen to human beings. Quran 57:22, "No disaster can ever befall the earth, neither your own selves, unless it be (laid down) in Our decree before We bring it in to being, verily all this is very easy for God."

57:23, "Know this, so that you may not despair over whatever good has escaped you, nor exult (unduly) over whatever good has come to you, for God does not love any of those who out of self-conceit act in a boastful manner."

The natural disasters that afflict the earth are according to the law of nature as decreed by God. The natural disasters like earthquakes, for example, are due to shifting of the earth's tectonic plates, flooding due to excess rains, tsunamis due to underwater volcanic eruptions, wildfires due to the sun's heat and lightning, etc. We have four seasons, which are very conspicuous in the West and mild in the Far East. This is due to the orbital pattern of the earth around the sun and the angle of earth's rotation on the long axis. So, all environmental phenomena that we experience on earth is due to an alteration in the orbital track of the planets and other natural changes in the earth's crust as determined by God in the law of nature.

Regarding diseases other than infection, deformities, and other personal disasters that affect human beings, these must be due to the mutations that occur in our DNA. The individual disasters and physical calamities referred to in the above verse are not related to worldly gains or losses, as in wealth or financial loss. In Islam, there is no correlation between faith and wealth. We can see that many Prophets were poor and suffered from lack of food. The case of Prophet Yusuf and his family is well known, in that Yusuf had to travel to the King of Egypt's court to work as a ration deliveryman, to earn a living.

We see that Prophet Muhammad had to starve on several occasions due to lack of provisions. Only Prophet Suleiman was a rich prophet. Therefore, the personal disasters referred to in the above verse must be physical, namely illness or death. The reference in the verse 57:22, "Unless it be in our decree," refers to our physical health, which is primarily determined by the DNA as devised by God. Health is of paramount importance to raise a family and health is determined by genes. The reason for these physical calamities and most diseases are dictated by the DNA and the genes and their mutations, and we call them fate or predetermination. But accidents, infections, poisoning, etc., are due to events occurring in the community and not due to genetic influence. Of course, some infections can have a genetic predilection.

From this, we can conclude that all these events on earth are preordained in the laws of nature and the personal disasters, diseases, and deformities are due to the function of DNA and its mutations, and not from random sporadic decisions from God. Indeed, all these are created by God, and we can ascribe all these happenings to God as well, but the distinction is that God did not make an on the spot decision either to punish or to favor a person, all are preordained or decreed in the law of nature and in our DNA and chromosomes. In the case of physical calamities of individuals, those which are directed by DNA can be altered due to the influence of epigenetics. Epigenetics means outside influence on the genetic expression without changing the genes.

Longevity can be extended by lifestyle modifications even though longevity is influenced by more than two hundred genes.

THE DOUBLE HELIX-DNA

There is a Hadith (saying of the prophet) in which the Prophet said that prayer (*dua*) is one factor that can increase one's longevity, attesting to the influence of epigenetics on gene expression as mentioned above.

Quran 5:48: "For each of you We have given a specific law (individually different and unique law) and a pattern of life. If God had willed He could have made you one people. But he wishes to try and test you by that which He gave you. So try to excel in good deeds, to Him will you all return in the end, when He will tell you of what you were at variance" (Ahmed Ali).

This verse has significant reference to our DNA and genes. The reference "to each of you a way and pattern of life" should not be interpreted as religious law. When God reveals a religion, it is meant for the entire community or the whole of mankind and not meant for an individual, even though an individual belongs to the community and follows the religion. Each one has been given a law, that should represent the law of life that is inscribed in the chromosome in the form of DNA and genes, and the law of life is the genetic code. Further, the verse says that God will give explanation for the dispute that human beings will have about the variance in them after death and resurrection. This may be a reference to the racial variance, physical and mental variance, that human beings will inherit and God will give explanation for it (at the time of the final judgement), whether due to allelic variations or otherwise. (Genetically speaking, alleles drive variations.) God says that if He willed, He could have made you all as one people. If it means that all individuals look alike without any identifying features other than male and female our race will be in great turmoil and confusion on earth. (Some exegetes indicate that it may mean tribes, race, etc.) We have over six billion people (human beings—the people referred to above) in the world and each one looks different, other than identical twins. Even children of the same parents do not look alike due to genetic variations (alleles). Alleles are alternative forms of the gene. Because of these alleles, six billion of us look different. During gene transfer from parents to children, each child gets half of his genes from his mother (twenty-three pairs) and half of his genes from his father (twenty-three pairs), for a total of forty-six pairs of chromosomes, and because the child inherits half of the genes from the mother and half from the father the offspring look different from either parent. Now the offspring has the full complement of DNA and genes and his life begins based on genetic information inscribed in the chromosomes in the form of DNA. This is a biological proof for predetermination on the basis of genetics. Because of God's limitless ingenuity through allelic alteration, each individual is phenotypically and genetically different from the other.

This verse further states to vie one another in doing virtuous deeds. Good deeds can change gene expression positively and will have beneficial outcomes as explained by epigenetics.

Here we have to read another verse from Quran: 49:13 which says "We have created you from a single pair of male and female and made you into people and communities that you may recognize each other. In order to recognize each other God has created us each with different features through this divine genetic alterations. The finger print is also unique for each individual. As described in the Quranic verse each individual is given a specific (uniquely different) law and pattern of life is the divine reference to our DNA which is specific for each individual. The finger print is also unique for each individual and that is why both DNA and finger prints are used to identify an individual in forensic medicine.

In 1880 Sir Francis Gold demonstrated that no two persons will have the exactly same finger print.

CHAPTER 21

Abrogation of the Divine Writ: The Torah, Bible (Injeel), and Quran vs. Genetic Mutation

Abrogation: There is some confusion with regard to the Verse, Quran 2;106, "Any message which We annul or confine to oblivion We replace with better or similar one." If we take it to mean some verses in Quran have been abrogated, then our faith in Islam will be shaken. We believe that God is all-knowing, and He will not have to change His mind so often. He knows the past, present, and the future and is all-knowing. For such a superpower, what is the need to change His message or abrogate? We cannot compare God to a human author who routinely changes the sentence or the message before it is finalized. The proponents of abrogation in Quran also claim that there are at least five verses that have been abrogated. This cannot happen as the Prophet would have taken out the verse that was abrogated. The only place we can agree about abrogation in divine writ is in terms of the messages in Torah and the Bible, which might have been misrepresented due to the method and timing of their collection, preservation, and recording, and those mistakes and omissions have been abrogated and corrected in Quran.

Quran 10:37, "Now this Quran could not possibly have been devised by anyone but God: nay indeed, it confirms the truth of whatever there still remains (of earlier revelations, Vedas, Torah and

Injeel-Bible) and clearly spells out the revelation (which comes) let there be no doubt about it from the sustainer of all the worlds."

This pattern of confirmation of previous revelation and corrections is reiterated in Quran, Sura 61:6 with regards to Torah "(and this happened too) when Jesus the son of Mary, said: O children of Israel? Behold I am an apostle of God unto you (sent) to confirm the truth of whatever there still remains of the Torah and to give (you) the glad tidings of an apostle who shall come after me, whose name shall be Ahmad."

Here we have to look at another Quranic verse 2:106, which says, "Whichever message we abrogate or cause to be forgotten (consign to oblivion) we bring one better than it or similar to it."

In this verse, God says He abrogates the message, which for a believer is hard to digest as God is all-knowing and has no reason to change a message whatsoever. One cannot consider God as an earthly author who needs to change a word or sentence willy nilly, and the all-knowing God will never change His instructions as and when needed. And the verse says God changes the message with a better one or one similar to it. If it means that the new one is better than the abrogated one, it also is inconsistent with the action of the Almighty whose decisions are final and do not need revision. The statement "one better or similar to it" needs some explanation. In this statement, "one similar to it" is not abrogation at all. When one abrogates a message, how can it be replaced with a similar one? These statements make one wonder that the meaning of this verse as explained by the commentators may not be correct. As we know, Arabic words can have five different meanings depending on the context and the situations. Sir Francis Gold demonstrated that no two persons will have exactly the same finger print. People ask how God can resurrect and identify individual after death? Quran 75: 3-4 "Does man think that We cannot (resurrect him and) bring his bones together again? Yea indeed We are able to make in complete order even his very finger tips!

Quran also directs us to use our judgment and reasoning, repeatedly to understand the meaning of the verses in Quran 8:22; 10:100. Therefore, we need to look at a different explanation and

THE DOUBLE HELIX-DNA

reasoning to understand the above mentioned verse of Quran. If we look at this verse in terms of biological evolution, our genome and DNA, our thoughts and confusion about the statement in the verse will clear up. As we know, since the appearance of the unicellular organism on earth about 3.5 billion years ago, there have been many additions to our genome in the form of different DNA due to mutations and many genes are replaced (abrogation) in our genome. Better and better genes (genetic messages) are added to the genome due to mutations in the biological evolution process and that is the reason for human beings to appear on earth (through evolution).

Quran 13:39, God annuls or confirms whatever He wills (of his earlier messages) for with Him is the source of all revelations. It is in the genome that old DNA is replaced by new and mutated DNA. The old ones are called the Junk DNA (comparison to the Quranic statement: message sent to oblivion).

Regarding using judgment and reasoning, Quran 8:22 says, "Verily the vilest of all creatures in the sight of God are those deaf and those dumb ones who do not use their reason."

10:100, "Not withstanding that no human being can ever attain to faith otherwise than by God's leave and it is He who lays the loathsome evil of disbelief upon those who will not use their reason."

Our genome contains 97 percent noncoding DNA or "Junk DNA." They were once functioning in lower species and have been sent to oblivion (abrogated) and replaced with new and better genes to function as human beings. Over billions of years God has written down in the DNA, mechanisms to have mutations to create different species including man. For this, the DNA would have to be changed and old ones would have to be made dysfunctional (abrogated) and new ones would have to be created (replaced with) since biological evolution is a continuous process of transformation and genetic alteration, species change from one to a different species. Because each species has a different genetic code (message) the genetic code (message) of previous species has to be abrogated and a new code (message) has to be formed, from one to the next species and a new, or better message (DNA) had to be inscribed in the chromosome, or a similar but functionally different genes (alleles) to be inserted.

But the divine revelation instructing as to how to lead a God-fearing life needs no change as it is meant for human beings and the community, who are stable as a species starting from the first human (Adam, Manu in Hindu philosophy) till the end of human existence. Whether it is the Vedas, Torah or Injeel, they are all from the same God for one purpose-to instruct human beings as to how to be God-fearing individuals. But in those scriptures, in the written form that is available, mistakes and omissions would have happened as the methods of recording and the preservation of the revelations were not as strict as was the case in Quran. And due to this possibility of omissions and mistakes, Quran was revealed correcting the omissions and abrogating the wrong segments of the inscriptions in those books (Torah and Injeel). This abrogation is not to be confused with the opinion of some commentators that certain Quranic verses were abrogated, which is untrue. The abrogation most likely refers to inserting new DNA (the mutated ones) into the existing species like the great apes and even the Nandearthals and abrogating or annulling the DNA or alleles of the previous species, to create human DNA and eventually the human beings and the new human genetic code in our genome.

The human genome is the repository of human genetic code (law of life) for our life and function. This process of inscription of the new code of life for the new baby takes place after fertilization, in the womb, and it is the essence of "predetermination" as described before. It has to be remembered that the basic genetic code that was transferred from the parents will continue with modifications into the new child. This basic law of life (genetic code) has continued unabatedly for over 3.5 billion years but DNA has changed considerably.

This genetic code (DNA) can be totally changed if God decides to transform the human species to a different species as described in Quran 56:61. That will be consistent with the Quranic statement (2:106): "Whichever message We abrogate or cause to be forgotten (consign to oblivion) We bring one better than it or similar to it."

Quran describes biological evolution in many verses (Adam's gene and Mitochondrial Eve). During biological evolution starting from the unicellular organism 3.5 billion years ago, several changes

THE DOUBLE HELIX-DNA

in the genome have occurred and several species have evolved and due to continued mutations of the beneficial variety, eventually human beings have appeared on earth about fifteen to twenty-five thousand years ago. In this evolutionary process, previously functioning DNA had to be abrogated or made dysfunctional and new and better DNA had to be added. In some cases alleles of genes, which is an alternative form of the gene will be introduced giving rise to different traits and small-scale evolution. These alleles are alternate forms of the genes similar to it with slight variation in base sequences. This relates to the Quranic expression of a message being replaced with a similar (allele) message. This Quranic description (2:106) aptly describes the biological evolutionary process ("similar one" refers to alleles and "better ones" refers to mutated variety). This cannot be interpreted as abrogating the Quranic verses or suras.

CHAPTER 22

Human Communication

It is not certain when the human species started communication skills. It is difficult to get a time line to establish when this happened. But archeologists have some idea about the earliest indication of human communication. It is believed that it happened in Africa or Asia from studies of fossils and cave dwellings.

From caves in Sothern France, carbon dating has shown that human beings lived there and paintings on the walls are believed to be about thirty to thirty-two thousand years ago. The Sumerians developed cuneiform writing on clay tablets, and it is believed to be the oldest full-fledged writing. The writing indicated it was to keep records of goods and supplies exchanged.

1050 BC—the Phoenicians developed the alphabet
900 BC—the Chinese used postal service for the government
305 BC—wooden printing press developed in China
1450—Newspaper appeared in Europe
1455—Guttenberg started metal typing and printing
1950—TV appeared
1994—Internet became available worldwide

Communication can be in gestures, sound, spoken words, tape, or CD recording, but we are now looking at the method of communication that the cells in our body use. This system started 3.5

billion years ago in the unicellular organism in the water. Then the multicellular organisms adopted it with additional features to incorporate more complicated genetic communication to produce more specialized proteins and enzymes to continue and sustain our life and evolve in to new species.

Even though the advanced species that we claim we are, we have not yet perfected a universal social communication system or a spoken language. There are over six thousand languages in the world and one cannot communicate in all of them. There is an elaborate system of communication in our body, in the human cell which is essential for our life and for maintaining life. This basic fundamental communication system has not changed in 3.5 billion years since the appearance of the unicellular organism, which is called the genetic code. The message might have changed in different species, but the basic system has not.

What a superb system, some will argue that the unicellular organism got it right accidentally, and that line of cells, multiplied and through the process of mutation and natural selection finally human beings came to existence. Others will claim that there must be a supernatural force, namely God behind it all.

Even though it is working in our body from conception till death, human beings still don't understand the full intricacy of this method of communication, which is responsible for our life and maintenance of our life and the principles and basics of this communication system have remained the same over 3.5 billion years. This is the language of our DNA in the chromosomes. This resides in the tiny cells in our body that can be seen only with advanced microscopes.

It is fascinating that we are exploring the universe, but knowing very little about our own body and its function.

This communication system that the DNA has devised (the genetic code) works in all living things both animals and plants, bacteria or viruses. That makes it a universal communicating system that will never be duplicated. It works in all parts of the world regardless of their spoken language.

CHAPTER 23

Conclusion

The universe and all its contents, including human beings, will come to an end as all are created with a plan including its end. Some of the life-forms like the vegetables, grain, and some perennials get dried up and die in front of our eyes. We can see the sprout, the fully grown plant, its fruition and eventually its death. By observing the plant one can make a prediction whether the crop will be good or bad. God, who can see and observe everything from the beginning or even before the beginning of the universe and till the end of the universe, knows every individual's behavior and activities till he dies. And He can make an evaluation based on a person's life, a report card as to whether the person will be in heaven or in hell, even before the individual's death. But this is not the final judgment that will come after the end of the world (Qiyama in Arabic). (Quran 3:185, Bible, Matthew:25:31-46). This judgment is based on the sum total of the good and bad deeds that the individual does and gets credit that he or she deserves. Therefore, doing good things always tends to earn favorable final judgment. The notion that our fate is already decreed, and there is no benefit in leading a good life is erroneous, as good deeds are divinely appreciated and rewarded, from a scientific aspect good deeds alter the genetic expression in the individual into being a social human being, from an antisocial one and this alters God's judgment.

Since we do not have a preview to the information on our divine report card, it is incumbent on every individual to be God-fearing and live a life of moderation and politeness. This fact, we, the human beings cannot comprehend as we cannot see the future, but God can. This also has bearing on the good Karma as in Hinduism and repentance (Dua in Arabic) as in Abrahamic religion. All these have influence on the genetic expression namely a vicious behavior pattern can be changed to a desirable one as discussed earlier. Since we do not know what is in our progress card created by God, and since we know that good deeds make our position more favorable we cannot sit idle saying my fate is already sealed, and I cannot change it. As discussed before, good deeds can change our fate.

We will limit our discussion to human beings. After the Homo sapiens emerged, the qualities that we ascribe to be human, have been set by DNA and genes. As discussed earlier our physical characteristics, internal organ function, our thought processes, all are determined by the DNA and this scientific fact is already existing in the human species long before our conception through the DNA of our parents. But allelic alterations can produce certain individual characteristics that make all of us different from the other, without changing the genes that give the basic qualities that make us human. That is the reason we can say that our fate or predetermination (al-Qadar in Arabic) to be human and behave like one and to experience life events has already been written or established in our genome long before we are born.

References

1. Telomere: Britt J. Heidinger; Jonathan O. Blount: PNAHS, August 15, 2011.
2. Quran 1:145, Asad.
3. Quran 57:22.
4. Quran 3:185.
5. Wikipedia.
6. Gregor Mendel.
7. DNA: James Watson and Francis Crick, 1953.
8. Charles Darwin.
9. Genome project, 2001.
10. The heavenly tablet, Quran 85:22.
11. Al Jibiriya.
12. Al Qadiriyya.
13. Sunni sect.
14. Tabari, Razi, Ibn Kathir.
15. Vedas, Torah, Bible (Injeel).
16. Leonardo Da Vinci. Fetal development. Fifteenth century AD.
17. Galen, on the formation of fetus.
18. Aristotle. Stages of chick embryo.
19. Anton Van Leeuwenhock. Seventeenth century. Microscope discovered.
20. Streeter. Stages of embryo. 1941.
21. O'Rhilly. Stages of embryo. 1972.
22. Quran. Fetal development.
23. Quran 4:133. New Race.

24. Discovery of cell. Robert Hooke. 1665.
25. Mathias Jacob Schneider and Theodore Schwab. Cell theory. 1839.
26. Sydney Brenner, et al, codon.
27. Annals of neurology. November, 2012. Harvard University
28. James Springer, James Lewis. Twin study.
29. Thomas Bouchard. University of Minnesota. Twin study.
30. Seventh-Day Adventist.
31. Greg Mendel.
32. Fred Griffin. Experiment with bacteri.
33. Oswald Avery, et al. DNA transforming factor.
34. Alfred Hershey, Martha Chase-Phage experiment.
35. Abrahamic religion, Zoroastrianism.
36. Karma, rebirth, Hinduism.
37. Quran 6:54. Falling leaf.
38. Quran 31:34. He knows what is in the womb.
39. Quran 32:11. The angel of death.
40. Quran 2:31. Taught names to Adam.
41. Quran 2:32. No knowledge save.
42. Quran 2:34. Angels prostrate before Adam.
43. Quran 17:70. Adam's sons above other creations.
44. Azrail, angel of death.
45. Bible 14:5. A person's days are determined.
46. Quran 7:34. For every people a term determined.
47. Qadar, fate.
48. Quran 3:144. Prophet either dies or slain.
49. Quran 35:11. The law of nature.
50. Foxo3, longevity gene.
51. Quran 57:22. Unless it is written down in our decree.
52. Quran 57:23. You may not despair.
53. Prophet Joseph.
54. Prophet Suleiman.
55. Quran 5:48. To each of you, we have given a law.
56. Southern France cave.
57. Sumerian writings.
58. Phenesians, 1050 BC. Alphabets.

THE DOUBLE HELIX-DNA

59. Chinese, 900 BC. Postal service.
60. 305 BC. Wooden printing press.
61. 1459. Newspaper in Europe.
62. 1455. Gutenberg metal typing.
63. 1950. TV appeared.
64. 1994. Internet
65. Al Qadar wal Qaeda. Divine decree.
66. Sixth pillar of faith.
67. Quran 39:6. Makes in the womb.
68. Cell membrane.
69. Cytoplasm.
70. Cytoskeleton.
71. Organelle.
72. Nucleus.
73. Chromosome.
74. Mitochondria.
75. Endoplasmic reticulum.
76. Golgi Apparatus.
77. Vesicles.
78. ATP.
79. Genetic code.
80. DNA.
81. Morse Code.
82. Qatar.
83. Quran 25:2.
84. Ibid., 36:38.
85. Ibid., 40:57.
86. Ibid., 13:2.
87. Ibid., 54:1.
88. Bible, Genesis 2:7.
89. Quran 23:12–14.
90. Quran 61:6.
91. Ibid., 5:48.
92. Wikipedia.
93. Genesis 5:5.
94. Genesis 6:3.

95. Quran 16:70.
96. Quran 30:54.
97. Quran 3:185.
98. Bible, Matthew 27:46.
99. Battle of Uhud.
100. Death of Umar (RA). Wikipedia.
101. Death of Caliph Uthman (RA). Wikipedia.
102. Death of Caliph Ali (RA).
103. Imam Hassan's (RA) death.
104. Death of Imam Hussain (RA).
105. Earthquake. Pakistan. 2005.
106. Bible, Job 14:5; Quran, 2:259, 6:60.
107. Journal of the National Cancer Institute, April 10, 2015.
108. Quran 3:18.
109. Quran 5:22, 10:100.
110. Bible. Biblical research Institute. Angel Manuel Rodrigues.
111. Sumerian and Akkadian papers.
112. Quran 85:22.
113. Quran 2:2; 2:106; 13:39.
114. Quran 35:11.
115. Quran 33:6.
116. Quran 18:109.
117. Quran 18:109. Yusuf Ali's comment on God's words.
118. Cool Cosmos, NASA.
119. Wikipedia.
120. Wikipedia.
121. Albert Einstein.
122. Ephesians 1:11
123. Psalm 139:13–16.
124. New Testament.
125. Acts 4:28.
126. Romans 8:29–30.
127. 1 Corinthians 2:7.
128. Ephesians 1:5.
129. Ephesians 1:11.

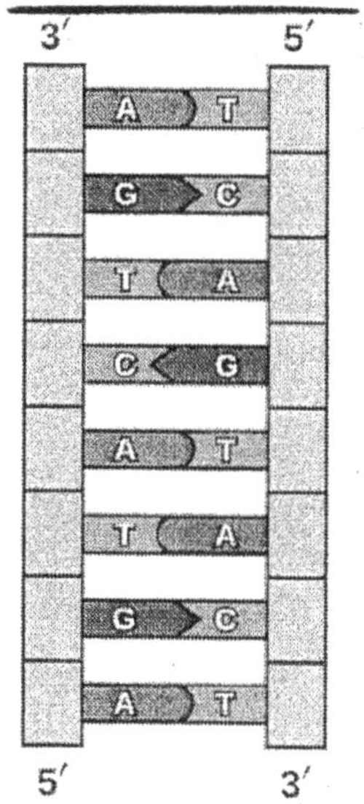
3′
5′
A
T
G
C
T
A
C
G
A
T
T
A
G
C
A
T
5′
3′

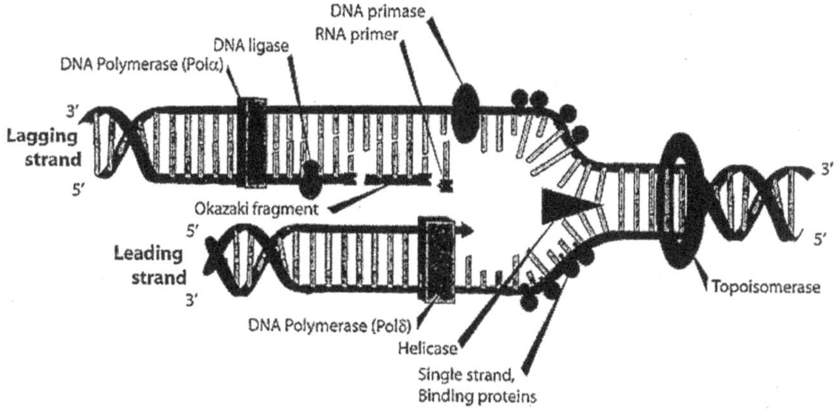
DNA primase
RNA primer
DNA ligase
DNA Polymerase (Polα)
3′
Lagging strand
5′
Okazaki fragment
5′
Leading strand
3′
3′
5′
Topoisomerase
DNA Polymerase (Polδ)
Helicase
Single strand, Binding proteins

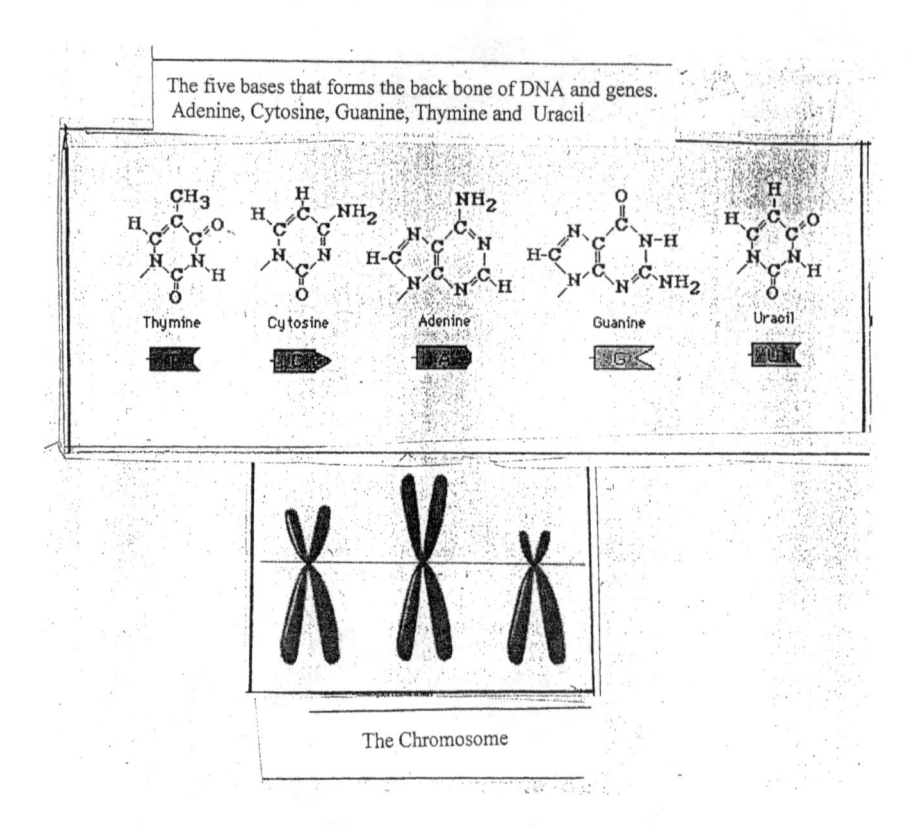

The five bases that forms the back bone of DNA and genes.
Adenine, Cytosine, Guanine, Thymine and Uracil

Thymine Cytosine Adenine Guanine Uracil

The Chromosome

Index

A

Abrahamic, **10**, **61**, **100**, **119**
Abrogation, **111**
Abu Sufiyan, 79
Acts 4:28, **15**
Ahmed Ali, 77
Alfred Hershey, **49**
Angel of Death, 74
angels, **103**, **104**
Annals of Neurology, **71**
Any message which We annul, **111**
Aristotle, 37
ATP, **32**, **33**, **36**
Azrail, **103**, **104**

B

Bible, **12**, **19**, **21**, **24**, **25**, **53**, **72**, **79**, **87**, **102**, **105**, **111**, **112**, **118**
Big Bang, **23**, **69**, **79**
body (soma), **43**
BRCA 1 or BRCA 2 gene, **89**
Bruce Lipton, **28**

C

caliph, 79
caliph Umar, 79
Calvinists, **16**
cell membrane, **28**, **32**, **33**
cell theory, **29**
Charles Darwin, **13**
Christianity, **15**, **69**

chromosomes, **13**, **19**, **32**, **41**, **43**, **45**, **47**, **48**, **50**, **51**, **52**, **57**, **60**, **61**, **62**, **63**, **68**, **69**, **73**, **74**, **76**, **90**, **103**, **104**, **106**, **108**, **110**, **117**
Chromosomes, **32**, **43**, **45**, **47**, **50**
codon, **33**
Colin McLeod, **49**
color, **13**, **43**, **48**, **60**, **61**, **64**, **78**
Corinthians, **15**
correction of Torah, **21**
Cro-Magnons, **68**
cytoplasm, **32**
cytoskeleton, **32**

D

deletion, **91**
divine decree, **11**, **77**, **100**
DNA, **5**, **10**, **13**, **14**, **19**, **20**, **24**, **25**, **27**, **28**, **29**, **32**, **33**, **38**, **41**, **43**, **45**, **47**, **48**, **49**, **50**, **51**, **52**, **53**, **55**, **56**, **57**, **60**, **61**, **62**, **65**, **67**, **68**, **69**, **71**, **72**, **73**, **74**, **76**, **78**, **79**, **80**, **81**, **82**, **87**, **89**, **90**, **91**, **105**, **106**, **108**, **109**, **110**, **113**, **114**, **115**, **117**, **119**, **120**

E

earthquake, **80**
end of the world, **118**
Endoplasmic reticulum, **33**
Ephesians 1:11, **16**
Ephesians 1:5, **15**

epigenetics, **6, 10, 14, 27, 28, 53, 61, 64, 69, 70, 81, 105, 108, 109, 110**
Esarhaddon, **22**

F

fetal development, **37, 38**
FOXO3, **47, 107**
Fred Griffin, **48**

G

Galen, **37**
gene expression, **28, 50, 60, 66, 70, 80, 81, 109, 110**
Genesis 2:7, **12**
Genesis 6:3, **72**
genetic code, **20, 25, 33, 35, 38, 41, 51, 52, 60, 66, 90, 100, 102, 105, 113, 114, 117**
Genetic code, **33**
G-G genotype, **72**
God, **5, 9, 10, 11, 12, 13, 15, 16, 18, 19, 20, 21, 22, 23, 24, 25, 26, 41, 42, 51, 52, 53, 60, 61, 64, 65, 67, 69, 73, 77, 78, 79, 80, 81, 87, 100, 101, 103, 104, 106, 107, 108, 109, 110, 111, 112, 113, 114, 117, 118, 119, 120**
God declares that Adam, **104**
Golgi Apparatus, **33**
Gosala, **17**
Gregor Mendel, **13**
Guttenberg, **116**

H

Hadith, **64, 102, 109**
Hafils, **20**
Hafiz, **19**
Haia, **22**
Hamza, **69**
Hassan ibn Ali, **80**

heavenly tablet, **19, 22, 23, 53**
Hinduism, **17, 26, 61, 69, 103, 105, 119**
Homo sapiens, **41, 50**
human cell, **29, 45, 47, 61, 65, 89, 117**
Human Genome, **50**

I

in pre-Islamic Arabia, **11**
in the form of epigenetics, **102**
Injeel, **19, 20, 21, 25, 111, 112, 114**
Internet, **116**
invisible forces, **65**
Islam does not believe in crucifixion, **79**
Islamic faith, **11, 24, 86, 105**

J

Jambavan and Satrajit, **69**
James Lewis, **67**
James Springer, **67**
James Watson, **5**
Jehovah's witness, **24**
Job 14:5, **105**
Judeo-Christian, **105**
Junk DNA, **113**

K

Kalifa, **104**
Karbala, **80**
karma, **10, 17, 26, 61, 87, 100**

L

law of nature, **23, 61, 62, 65, 79, 80, 81, 106, 107, 108**
Leonardo da Vinci, **37**
Life never dies, **42**

M

Martha Chase, **49**

Matthias Jacob Schneider, **29**
microscope, **37**
Missense mutation, **91**
mitochondria, **47**, **91**
Mitochondria, **32**
Morse code, **35**
mRNA, **33**, **57**, **60**, **90**
Muharram, **80**
Muslim aqidah, **18**
mutation, **41**

N

NASA, **28**
Neanderthals, **68**
New Testament, **15**
Newspaper, **116**
Niyati, **17**
No calamity can ever befall, **23**, **77**
Nonsense mutation, **91**
nucleus, **13**, **14**, **29**, **32**, **33**, **43**, **47**, **50**, **51**, **53**, **56**, **63**, **74**, **90**, **91**

O

O'Rahilly, **37**
on biochemical principles, **35**
organelle, **32**
Oswald Avery, **49**

P

Pay Zakath, **26**
Phoenicians, **116**
Predestination, **9**, **15**, **17**, **18**
Prince Rim-Sin a reign, **22**
Prophet, **20**, **21**, **64**, **65**, **69**, **79**, **80**, **102**, **105**, **106**, **108**, **109**, **111**
Prophet Suleiman, **108**

Q

Qadar, **73**
fate, **11**, **12**, **18**, **19**, **60**, **62**, **65**, **66**, **73**, **78**, **87**, **100**, **105**, **119**
Qatar, **24**, **53**

Quran 1:145, **77**
Quran 13:11, **80**
Quran 13:2, **12**
Quran 13:39, **113**
Quran 16:70, **73**
Quran 17:70, **104**
Quran 18:109, **51**
Quran 2:2, **22**
Quran 23:12, **64**
Quran 23:13, **38**
Quran 25:2, **11**
Quran 3:144, **106**
Quran 3:18, **118**
Quran 3:185, **77**
Quran 31:34, **64**
Quran 32:11, **103**
Quran 33:6, **23**
Quran 35:11, **22**, **106**
Quran 39:6, **37**
Quran 4:133, **42**
Quran 40:57, **12**
Quran 5:48, **21**, **109**
Quran 56:61, **114**
Quran 57:22, **23**, **77**, **107**
Quran 6:2, **77**
Quran 6:59, **61**
Quran 61:6, **20**
Quran 8:22, **113**
Quran 85:22, **18**
Quran and Bible, **87**

R

radioactive phosphorus, **49**
radioactive sulfur, **49**
Ramadan, **80**
RAS, **25**
rebirth, **100**
religion of Islam is based on five fundamental creeds, **26**
Repeat expansion, **91**
reticular activating system, **25**
Robert Hooke, **29**
Romans, **15**, **87**

RUH, **24, 25, 103**

S

schizophrenia, **68, 89**
sixth pillar, **11**
Soul and Ruh, **24**
SRY, **63**
Streeter, **37**
Sumerian document, **22**
Sydney Brenner, **33**

T

Tabari, **19**
Telomere, **22, 71, 74, 76, 87**
Tesla, **27**
The Heavenly Tablet, **21**
the soul, **18, 24, 26, 81, 101, 102, 103**
the transforming principle, **49**
Theodore Schwab, **29**
Thomas Bouchard, **67**
time keeper of death, **87**
time of death, **72, 103**

Torah, **19, 20, 21, 24, 25, 111, 112, 114**
TV appeared, **116**

V

vedas, **111**
Vedas, **19, 114**
vibrational strings, **27**
Vikarma, **17**
Vivekananda, **17**

W

was crucified, **79**
William Oschner, **89**

X

XX female, **62**

Z

Zoroastrianism, **61**
zygote, **37**

About the Author

Dr. Kutty is a physician practicing the subspecialties of pulmonary/critical care and sleep medicine. My hobby is reading about religion and science and trying to see if there is any scientific correlation for the religious doctrines. In my first book *Adam's Gene and the Mitochondrial Eve*, I have demonstrated that Adam and Eve, the first two human beings according to Judeo, Christian, and Islamic faiths were the result of evolution rather than creation. In this book, I have shown that our destiny is determined by our genes and DNA and not due to random decision by the Almighty God.